DAIMLER DIGEST

DB18 AND CONQUEST RANGES
(1945-1957)

Compiled by
DANIEL YOUNG

1990
Published and distributed by
P4 Spares
60 Woodville Road
London NW11 9TN
(01-455 6992)

ISBN 0 9511760 9 9

Preface

The remarkable growth of the classic car movement in recent years has been clearly reflected in the impressive variety of books currently in print on every aspect of that subject. It is surprising, therefore, that marques such as Daimler and Lanchester have been sadly neglected, leaving enthusiasts of cars of such excellence with so little reading material available to them today.

This modest offering, along the lines of the Rover Anthology (6 vols), published by ourselves since 1986, is an attempt to bridge this gap. The present volume concentrates on the 2½-litre post-war Daimlers, the DB18 and Conquest ranges. A further volume is available, covering the big Daimlers (3-litre upwards) up to and including the DS420 limousine introduced in 1968, which is still a current model. A volume on post-war Lanchester cars is in preparation.

We have included road tests, new model descriptions, numerous period advertisements and the *Motor Trader* Service Data for the Conquest series. Some information in the latter item may now require updating but it nevertheless remains an interesting document for Conquest owners.

I would like to thank Brooklands Books, the undisputed pioneers of road test collections, for their unfailing support; the Daimler and Lanchester Owners' Club for their advice and encouragement — in particular Mr C. David Adcock, Club President, for the loan of his rare photographs and publicity copy; also *Autocar*, *Motor* and *Motor Trader*, the sources of the material reproduced here.

A further volume on Lanchester cars is currently in preparation.

Finally, it is hoped that enthusiasts will derive many enjoyable hours of reading from this collection.

D.Y.

Daimler and Lanchester Owners Club Ltd. membership details available from:
John Ridley
The Manor House
Trewyn
Abergavenny
Gwent NP7 7PG
Telephone: (0873) 890737 (office)

Cover illustration:
The Conquest Century Saloon as shown in the official sales literature.

3

Behind the wheel of this car you will usually find a

man who has learned to know and love a fine machine.

BY APPOINTMENT

THE   DAIMLER   COMPANY   LTD   ·   LONDON   AND   COVENTRY

B

FLUID DRIVE
NOW ADOPTED BY AMERICA

Today 'fluid drive' is all the fashion in America. All the leading makes there are fitting it — and proclaiming it too! It was Daimler who discovered, developed and by 1930 perfected, this wonderful system of Fluid Transmission. *The whole aspect of driving is changed, simplified, by Fluid Transmission.* Naturally your new Daimler will have Fluid Transmission — and what a magnificent car it will be!

BY APPOINTMENT

Daimler

18

Daimler-Lanchester Plans

Advance Details of the New Programme

FIRST of the Daimler range to make its appearance will be the Fifteen. This has the 2½-litre six-cylinder engine which proved highly successful during the war in the Daimler Scout car, and as a result of the experience thus gained a number of improvements have taken place and will be incorporated in the Fifteen, delivery of which is expected to commence in a matter of weeks.

The modifications which have been made have resulted in greatly improved engine efficiency with a higher b.h.p. output and a fuel consumption estimated to be 25 per cent. better than that of the pre-war model, a figure of 21.6 m.p.g. having been obtained on test at an average speed of 50 m.p.h.

Features of the new six-light saloon body are thin pillars to allow the maximum of vision for all occupants, greater width for more comfortable seating, and improved luggage accommodation. The body is metal framed and use is made of laminated wood to obtain the desired curvature.

Among interesting chassis features are independent front-wheel suspension, automatic chassis lubrication, and built-in mechanical jacking. Fluid transmission will, of course, continue to be a feature of both the Daimler and the Lanchester ranges.

The programme will also include the 27 h.p. six-cylinder and 36 h.p. eight-cylinder models, some examples of which are expected to be available early in the New Year.

As regards the Lanchester, an entirely new 10 h.p. four-cylinder model is in production, with pressed-steel coachwork, independent front-wheel suspension, and a number of engine refinements which have resulted in increased power and lower fuel consumption. Increased luggage accommodation is another good point. Delivery of this model will commence towards the end of the year. Production is also commencing of a 14 h.p. six-cylinder model, delivery to be early in 1946.

The latest Daimler Fifteen standard six-light saloon has a well-balanced appearance. Excellent visibility is obtained by the use of thin pillars. A large luggage locker is provided.

Compiler's note: Period magazine captions were not always accurate. Readers will note that two of the three cars shown on this page are incorrectly titled.

DAIMLER DELIVERIES

The 4½-litre Daimler limousine seen above was presented to H.H. The Aga Khan by his followers on the occasion of his recent Diamond Jubilee. On the right are some of the lavish interior fittings, which include radio, foot warmer, and electrically operated blinds. Below is the 3½-litre sports model which accompanied the 4½-litre and was used by H.H. Prince Ali Khan during the celebrations.

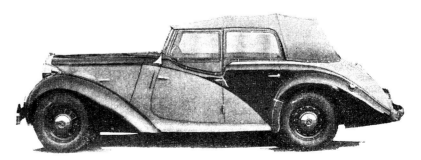

An Improved 2½-litre Daimler

DAIMLER 2½-LITRE DATA
(Letters in brackets refer to footnotes.)

	2½ Litre
Present tax	£22 10s.
Cubic capacity	2,522 c.c.
Cylinders	6
Valve position	Overhead
Bore	69.6 mm.
Stroke	110.49 mm.
Comp. ratio	7 to 1
Max. power (A) ..	70 b.h.p.
at	4,200 r.p.m.
Max. torque (A) ..	109 lb./ft.
at	2,000 r.p.m.
H.P.: Sq. in. piston area (A)	1.98
Wt.: Sq. in piston area (B)	98.2 lb.
Ft./Min. Piston speed at max. h.p. (A)	3,060
Carburetter	S.U. horizontal 1½ throttle
Ignition	Coil and distributor
Plugs: Make and type	Lodge CB14
Fuel pump	A.C. mechanical type
Oil filter make (by-pass, full flow)	Tecalemit full flow
Oil circulation: Galls. per min.	6
Clutch	Fluid flywheel
1st gear	4.08 to 1
2nd gear	2.32 to 1
3rd gear..	1.56 to 1
Top gear	1 to 1
Reverse	5.4 to 1
Prop. shaft	Hardy Spicer
Final drive	8/35
Brakes	Girling mechanical
Drums	11 in. dia.
Friction lining area ..	120 sq. in.
Car wt. per sq. in. (B)	28.9 lb.
Suspension	Independent front with coil springs Rear, half elliptic Luvax piston-type shock-absorbers
Steering gear	Marles
Steering wheel (dia.) ..	18 in. adjustable
Wheelbase	9 ft. 6 in.
Track, front	4 ft. 4 in.
Track, rear	4 ft. 4 in.
Overall length	15 ft. 0 in.
Overall width	5 ft. 4½ in.
Overall height	5 ft. 3 in.
Ground clearance ..	6 in.
Turning circle	41 ft.
Weight—dry	31 cwts.
Tyre size	6.00×16
Wheel type	Spoked disc
Fuel capacity	14 gallons
Oil capacity	1 gallon 3 pints
Water capacity.. ..	3 gallons 2 pints
Electrical system ..	12 volt c.v.c.
Battery capacity ..	69 amps. at 20 hrs.

Top Gear Facts:

Engine speed per 10 m.p.h.	510 r.p.m.
Piston speed per 10 m.p.h.	367 f.p.m.
Road speed at 2,500 ft./min. (piston) ..	67.5 m.p.h.
Litres per ton-mile (B)	2,500

(A) With normal setting of carburetter, etc.
(B) Dry weight.

An Attractive Six-light Saloon of Interesting Construction with Commodious Accommodation

WITH the experience of no less than 50 successful years of motorcar manufacture behind them, and profiting by experience gained in manufacture of light scout cars during the recent war, the Daimler company have made a number of interesting modifications to the 2½-litre model for 1946. Many of these are mechanical, but, in addition, there is an entirely new and attractive body style; the combination will, undoubtedly, have a particular appeal to those who look for a car with good performance yet possessing that element of individuality and dignity with which the name of Daimler has always been associated.

In many respects the chassis remains unchanged from earlier models of this type. The frame is still of straightforward and robust design, with U-section side members and cruciform cross bracing. Front suspension is the normal Daimler I.F.S., incorporating heavy-duty coil springs, while that at the rear is by long semi-elliptics. Both front and rear are controlled by Luvax piston-type shock absorbers, those at the front being coupled by an anti-roll bar. The result is very smooth riding coupled with complete stability.

Completely mechanical Girling braking is fitted, with 11-in. brake drums to all wheels, and has proved by experience to be eminently satisfactory. The compensating mechanism has self-lubricating bushes and frequent maintenance of these points is thereby rendered unnecessary.

Improved Head Design

It is when one comes to the power unit that the improvements which have been made to this model become really apparent. To begin with, there is a completely redesigned cylinder head, in which the pushrod-operated valves are now set at an angle of 15 degrees. The shape of the combustion space and ports has been considerably modified, as will be seen in the sectioned view of the engine on another page. The resulting improvement in gas flow and turbulence has enabled a step-up to be made in compression ratio from 5.5 : 1 to 7 : 1 and has resulted in a power increase from 64 b.h.p. at 4,000 r.p.m. to 70 b.h.p. at 4,200 r.p.m. Notwithstanding this added output, the makers claim that petrol consumption has been improved to over 22 m.p.g., compared to the previous average figure of 18.

Another feature which has a direct bearing upon both power and petrol consumption is the redesigned induction pipe, which is now surrounded for its entire length by an integral cast water jacket connected to the main cooling system by a by-pass from the thermostat. When starting from cold, the thermostat remains closed and the warmed water from around the cylinder head commences its circulation in the direction where it will do most good.

A31

As a result, warming up is very rapid. At the other end of the temperature range, a slight reverse thermo-siphon action occurs, so that, under conditions of high engine temperature, the heat of the induction pipe is, to an extent, controlled. Carburation is by a single S.U. which is fed from a 14-gallon tank by a mechanical fuel pump driven off the camshaft.

Cooling is by pump and fan, the former being another redesigned component. Pump drive is by belt from the crankshaft pulley, the same belt driving the dynamo. At this point it is interesting to note the detail attention which has been given to ensuring a completely silent engine, in that the pulley angles have all been altered to prevent any possibility of belt squeak.

Special attention has been paid to valve-cooling and the water-jacketing arranged so that water passing from the cylinder block to the head is deflected through jets into close proximity of the exhaust-valve seats, which, incidentally, are inserts of hard iron alloy.

Engine lubrication is by gear pump from a sump holding 11 pints and, to ensure inner cleanliness, all oil passes at 40 lb. pressure through an external oil filter, on the outside of which is a pressure release valve.

Over-riding Control

Ignition is by normal battery and coil, with automatic advance and retard, but for the benefit of those touring abroad where widely varying grades of

The new six-light coachwork appears nicely balanced and, although roomy, does not give any impression of bulkiness.

The straightforward design of the Daimler chassis is apparent from this drawing, in which is also seen the water - cooled induction pipe, independent front suspension and built-in jacking system.

fuel may have to be used, there is an over-riding manual control by means of which the ignition setting can be varied so that pinking will not occur.

A Daimler feature for many years has been the employment of a fluid flywheel and preselector gearbox. Both these units are retained in this latest model, but the fluid flywheel has been modified by the elimination of the annular ring on the rotating members. As a result, it has been found that a better grip is obtained at low r.p.m., with consequent improvement in acceleration.

The preselector gearbox (with craft top gear ratio of 4.375 to 1) remains

The novel form of window channelling used on the new coachwork enables the width of the door and screen pillars to be reduced considerably and provides unusually good visibility.

generally unchanged. Selection is made by the usual quadrant situated on the steering column just below the steering wheel. Power is transmitted to the rear axle by an open propeller shaft with Hardy Spicer needle bearing joints at each end, and the axle is of the three-quarter floating type, with underslung rear drive.

Considerable attention has been paid to the needs of servicing and maintenance Chassis lubrication is completely automatic to all but six points, and these are very easily reached, either from outside the car or via small trapdoors in the floor. The radiator and front mudwing mounting is so designed that in the event of detail engine attention being required all that is necessary is to undo the water pipe clips and two nuts, which are easily reached,

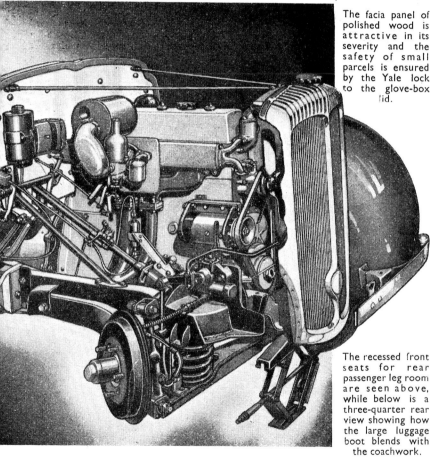

The facia panel of polished wood is attractive in its severity and the safety of small parcels is ensured by the Yale lock to the glove-box lid.

The recessed front seats for rear passenger leg room are seen above, while below is a three-quarter rear view showing how the large luggage boot blends with the coachwork.

Mulliners of Birmingham. It possesses many interesting features, primary among which is the employment of steel body members.

As a result of this form of construction, it has been found possible, by reducing the thickness of the actual body sides, to obtain a marked increase in accommodation without making the car appear unduly wide. It has also enabled thin body pillars to be used

when the entire assembly can be lifted clear after the bolts securing the wings to the chassis have been removed.

A built-in D.W.S. jacking system facilitates wheel-changing and the operating rods are located where it is not necessary to grovel in the dirt in order to reach them.

Steering is by Marles worm and double roller; the steering column is adjustable for length and is fitted with an 18-in. steering wheel. The resultant steering lock is 41 ft., which is reasonable for a car of this size.

The standard body fitted to the 2½-litre Daimler is an attractive six-light saloon with sunshine roof built by

A33

The 2½-litre Daimler—Contd.

without weakening the construction and thus give excellent all-round visibility.

Some idea of the roominess of the new coachwork will be appreciated when it is realized that the width of the rear seat at waist height is no less than 53½ ins. and that of the front only 1½ ins. less. Additional legroom is given to rear-seat passengers by recess-

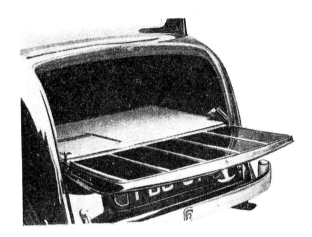

The composite bulk-head which forms a rigid scuttle mounting is shown above, while on the left is the capacious luggage compartment, of which the lid serves as an additional carrier.

ing the backs of the front seats, as will be seen from an illustration.

Running boards have been dispensed with and the doors open almost the entire depth of the body.

At the front end, the body is secured to a stout bulkhead of laminated wood faced with aluminium, which, in its turn, is secured to the chassis by really massive brackets. In this manner a completely rigid scuttle mounting is

achieved, which will undoubtedly have an effect upon body condition after considerable mileage has been covered.

The interior is upholstered in leather with fillets of polished wood. The somewhat severe facia panel is also of hardwood, a feature of which is a substantial Yale lock on the lid of the glove box. Large-dial instruments are fitted in positions where they can be easily read. In the centre is the winding

mechanism for opening and closing the windscreen.

The rear compartment is equipped with twin interior lights, controlled by switches set within easy reach of either front or rear seat occupants.

At the rear of the car there is a capacious luggage locker, the lid of which is designed to form an additional luggage platform and is fitted with runners and flush-fitting strap attachments. Underneath is a separate compartment for the spare wheel and tools, of which the panel is attached by an extensible hinge, permitting it to come away sufficiently for the spare wheel to be withdrawn and still remain attached to the car.

On a short run, while no actual data was obtained, the impression was formed that the 2½-litre Daimler will enhance still more the reputation of a company whose name has ever been associated with really good cars.

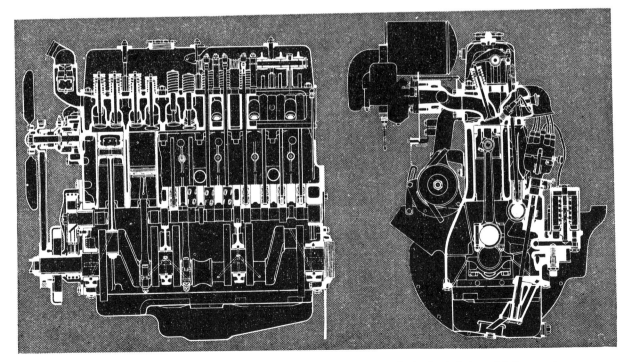

Side and end sections of the modified Daimler engine. The new cylinder-head design with improved porting and combustion space is clearly seen. The engine now develops 70 b.h.p. at 4,200 r.p.m.

DAIMLER

DB.18   2½ litre
Chassis 50050 to 53749
1946-49

MODEL	FRONT AND REAR BRAKES
DB.18 2½ litre Chassis 50040 to 53749 1946-49	11 × 1½ GNS Section 2, Page 1

Drop Head Coupe by Charlesworth

Abridged Specification — Drop Head Coupe by Charlesworth

First class coachbuilt construction with composite framing of best ash and plywood ; aluminium body panels ; one piece top-hinged windscreen; ventilating windows in both doors ; spring operated folding head to collapse into a recess behind rear backrest with an intermediate 'DeVille' position arranged by hinged cant rails that fold across body; adjustable front seats with easy access to full width rear seat; superior grade leather upholstery; solid walnut cabinet work ; polished fillet surrounds to screen and doors ; all fittings in best quality chrome plating ; large luggage boot with bottom hinged lid and separate compartment for spare wheel and tool kit.

Abridged Specification — Drop Head Coupe by Abbott

Constructed of best quality ash framing, panelled in aluminium ; single panel sloping winder type windscreen hinged at top; two wide doors hinged on rear pillars and fitted with anti-draught windows; hand operated, spring balanced folding head of fully open or fully closed type; adjustable bench type front seat with folding arm rest and hinged back for easy access to rear compartment in which one off-side mounted occasional seat faces across body ; best quality leather upholstery; cabinet work, fillets, window surrounds and panels on door tops in polished walnut; valance skirt fitted to rear wings; large luggage boot with lid to open upwards and separate locker for spare wheel and tool kit.

Drop Head Coupe by Abbott

COACHWORK DE LUXE
by
TICKFORD

DAIMLER TICKFORD D.H. COUPE

LONDON SHOWROOMS :
TICKFORD LTD. 6-9 UPPER SAINT MARTIN'S LANE, LONDON W.C.2
WORKS : NEWPORT PAGNELL · BUCKS.

The Daimler 2½-litre Saloon

A Medium-sized Car of Real Distinction

PRODUCED by one of Britain's oldest-established motorcar manufacturers, the Daimler 2½-litre displays an unusual blend of qualities. On the one hand, it offers the comfort and refinement which is expected of a car carrying the fluted Daimler radiator. On the other hand, however, it provides the lively performance and responsive controls which are more often associated with the best products of continental factories. It is a car which should appeal strongly to motoring enthusiasts of matured tastes.

In general layout a very practical car, the Daimler is at its best when providing luxurious transport for four people. Loaded thus, everyone has ample leg and elbow room, the front passenger having the advantage of a seat which is adjustable independently of the driving seat. The vision from all seats is quite exceptionally good, thanks to the narrow roof pillars and generously proportioned windows, and it is hard to find criticisms more serious than that the rear-seat central armrest is set rather high.

As befits a car of its size, the body is also capacious enough to accommodate extra passengers when the need arises. The front seats can be set together to accommodate three people forming a satisfactory bench seat; the hand-brake and gear-lever are both situated on the right-hand side of the car, and a third person in the front compartment does not impede the driver's control of the car. The back seat also provides accommodation for three people, although the width between the wheel arches is scarcely adequate for real comfort.

When a car is fully loaded, there are inevitably many miscellaneous items of personal equipment to be carried. On this car the luggage boot is of very generous size, and the potential capacity is increased by a sturdy lid which folds down flat to extend its floor. The spare wheel and tool kit, incidentally, are locked away in a separate compartment and do not encroach upon the luggage accommodation. Inside the car, a lockable dashboard cubby hole provides safe stowage for such valuables as cameras, and there are pockets on all doors.

The four doors of the Daimler body are of useful size, and the whole floor of the car is flat. The neat walnut facia board has all the controls and instruments located within easy sight and

reach of the driver, and an ashtray is provided for each passenger. The windscreen can be opened for driving in fog, there is a scuttle ventilator, and, of course, a sliding roof; surprising, however, is the absence of any means of securing draught-free and rain-free ventilation.

For passengers, the 2½-litre Daimler must be judged as a delightful car in which to ride. Progress is smooth and peaceful, the scenery is in full view, and the car reaches its destination in quick time without feeling to hurry. It would somehow seem a waste to buy this model and hand it over to a chauffeur, however, for it is difficult to name any car which is more pleasant to drive.

Sure-footed

The springing is soft and the car can readily be rocked by hand when stationary. Our test included city streets and country lanes which had suffered severely from frost and floods, and the car always rode comfortably, although perhaps with not quite the exaggerated softness which is favoured on transatlantic models. An unplanned test for the suspension system was provided when a large lorry dropped its spare wheel flat in the roadway—the result being quite a mild bump as the car rode over an obstacle which was actually too high for mudguard damage to be avoided.

In open country, high speed actually seems to improve the riding comfort, and road irregularities of horrifying aspect can be completely ignored. Many

readers will know the open stretch of the Great West Road, A 30, which runs straight across Hartford Bridge Flats, and the bumps which have been formed by work on Blackbushe aerodrome— at a steady 70 m.p.h. with the car fully loaded, they were hardly perceptible to either front or rear passengers.

Flexible though the springs are, they are very adequately controlled by the hydraulic shock absorbers. The car does not apparently resonate and bounce under any conditions we encountered, and when a hump-back bridge is taken fast it rises, then sinks again and steadies itself without any tendency for spring movement to persist.

When a car is sprung for comfort, and built with a body high enough to be really comfortable, most people expect some roll on corners. The Daimler is certainly sprung for comfort, yet of lateral movement on bends there is hardly a trace. The car has to be cornered at speeds which would do credit to a sports car before tyre scream can be induced, and remains perfectly steady under such brutal treatment.

Although the car is appreciably heavier than the average run of British models, it has been endowed with steering which would be a credit to a much smaller vehicle. Geared at 2⅔ turns from lock to lock, the turning circle is sufficiently compact to allow the car to be swung round in a wide road. In normal driving the wheel movement required is extremely moderate, yet the steering is also notably light, despite ample self-centring action.

VELVET GLOVED.—The engine of the Daimler is notably accessible. Overhead valves and a dual exhaust system contribute to an effortless maximum speed of over 70 m.p.h.

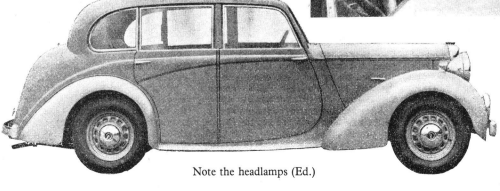

Note the headlamps (Ed.)

VISIBILITY.—Like a modern house, the car has really large windows, and is planned to provide every amenity within moderate overall dimensions.

A 31

The Daimler 2½-litre—Contd.

In general handling, the car responds beautifully to the helm; there is, perhaps, a trace of oversteer to account for the ease with which the Daimler will swing along winding roads, yet on the straight the driver does not consciously have to direct the car. After a 300-mile drive, much of it at a hurried pace and over secondary roads, a driver can become very critical of a car, and the Daimler gained full marks on all scores but one.

In saying that the car offers certainly as good a combination of comfort and good handling characteristics as any model we know, a proviso must, unfortunately, be made. The brakes we do

able to put itself at the front of most bunches of traffic. It should, perhaps, be recorded that, for the timing of acceleration from rest through the gears, the car was started on the fluid flywheel, the smooth getaway contrasting with the fiercer method needed if the best acceleration is to be obtained with an orthodox transmission. The maximum speed of the car is comfortably in excess of 70 m.p.h., this speed being attainable even in the teeth of a strong

FRONT COMFORT.—The individual front seats may be set together to provide accommodation for three people. Instruments, gear selector and hand-brake are all concentrated on the driver's side of the car.

BOXROOM.—The capacious luggage locker can be supplemented by folding the lid down to extend its floor. Tools and the spare wheel are accommodated separately in a lower compartment.

not regard as worthy of the car, the pedal effort required to effect a sudden stop from the high cruising speeds one is otherwise tempted to use being altogether too high. At no time was there any question of instability, even when the brakes were used forcibly at 70 m.p.h.

It is, perhaps, an unconscious tribute to the Daimler that, in writing about the car, it is easy to forget about the engine. The six-cylinder overhead-valve power unit started promptly from cold, and, with use of the enrichment control, would immediately get down to work. Under the weather conditions of our test, response to the throttle became normal in approximately a mile.

Hydraulic Drive

As for many years past, the fluid flywheel transmission is used, a preselective four-speed gearbox forming part of a system which has been fully proved both before and during the war. Before starting from rest, first or second gear may be selected, and engaged by depressing and releasing the clutch pedal. When the hand-brake is released and the throttle opened, the car moves smoothly and steadily forward, the amount of slip in the fluid flywheel diminishing as the engine speed rises. Other gears are similarly preselected by the steering-column lever, then engaged by depressing and releasing the pedal.

The acceleration figures printed on page 210 make it amply clear that the car is extremely lively, well

A32

wind. So effortless is the running at all times that it is almost impossible to specify a cruising gait—certainly continuous travel at something over the mile-a-minute causes neither driver, passengers, nor car any concern. It must be said, however, that the amount of gear and other noise audible during town driving is greater than is expected in a Daimler.

At night the main head lamps provide a very satisfactory driving light. The dipping switch, however, cuts out both head lamps in favour of a flat-beam lamp, and although this scheme has merit in misty weather, the dipped beam sometimes feels inadequate for fine-weather driving on main roads. The instrument lighting is extremely good, the body interior light may be switched on or off from either side of the car, and the rear lights remain visible when the rear lockers are open.

Although buyers in this country are unlikely to take a car such as the Daimler off metalled roads, good ground clearance in the right places is important in many parts of the world. On this model we found that there was no ten-

dency for any part of the car to ground on rough going, the rear overhang of the body being moderate and such items as exhaust tail pipes well clear of the ground. Taking up the drive gently, the fluid flywheel should assist traction on slippery surfaces, although any wheel-spin is not easily detected.

In mechanical matters, the Daimler 2½-litre is an extremely fine car, not, perhaps, revolutionary, but a most successful combination of the best modern design features. The bodywork, too, although conservative in styling and not entirely silent at all times, is well worthy of the car. Equipment is comprehensive, including such details as a manual override control for the ignition timing and a radiator thermometer, although, surprisingly, a warning lamp replaces the oil-pressure gauge.

In sum, we feel that, by present-day standards, the car represents very excellent value at the price of £1,304. Offering attractions to any motorist who can afford a medium-sized quality car, its strongest appeal is undoubtedly to the driver who can appreciate genuine mechanical excellence.

The Motor Road Test No. 4/47

Make : Daimler   **Type :** 2½-litre Saloon

Makers : The Daimler Co. Ltd., Coventry

Dimensions and Seating

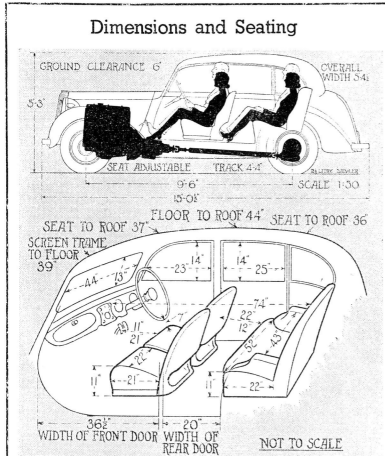

In Brief

Price £1,020
plus Purchase Tax £284 1s. 8d. =
                  £1,304 1s. 8d.

Tax	£26
Road weight unladen.. ..	31 cwt.
Laden weight as tested ..	34 cwt.
Consumption	22 m.p.g.
Speed	72.2 m.p.h.

(mean both ways)
57 m.p.h. 3rd
38 m.p.h. 2nd

Acceleration .. 10-30 on top, 13.7 secs.
0-50 through gears, 17.9 secs.

Tapley lb. per ton and
gradients : 175 lb. max. on top=1 in 13
275 lb. max. on 3rd=1 in 8
370 lb. max. on 2nd=1 in 6

Gearing .. 18.3 m.p.h. in top at 1,000
r.p.m. 63 m.p.h. at 2,500 ft.
per min. piston speed

Specification

Cubic capacity	2,522 c.c.
Cylinders	6
Valve gear	Pushrod o.h.v.
Bore	69.6 mm.
Stroke..	110.5 mm.
Compression ratio	7.0
Max. power	70 b.h.p.
at	4,200 r.p.m.
H.P. per sq. in. piston area ..	1.98
H.P. per ton, unladen ..	45.0
Piston area per ton, unladen	23.0
Litres per laden ton-mile ..	2,440
Ft./min. piston speed at max.	
h.p.	3,050
Carburetter	S.U. horizontal
Ignition	Lucas coil
Plugs : make and type ..	Lodge CB14
Fuel pump	A.C. mechanical
Oil filter	Tecalemit, full-flow
Clutch..	Fluid flywheel, with preselective gearbox
Top gear	4.375
3rd gear	6.84
2nd gear	10.17
1st gear	17.85
Reverse	23.6
Propeller shaft	Hardy Spicer
Final drive	Underslung worm
Brakes..	Girling mechanical
Brake drum diameter ..	11 ins.
Friction lining area	127 sq. ins.
Friction area per ton, unladen	82 sq. ins.
Steering gear	Marles
Tyre size	6.00 × 16

Test Conditions

Wet concrete, side wind gusting to gale force, Pool petrol, synthetic rubber tyres.

Test Data

ACCELERATION TIMES on Two Upper Ratios

	Top	3rd
10–30 m.p.h. ..	13.7 secs.	8.6 secs.
20–40 m.p.h. ..	14.1 secs.	8.7 secs.
30–50 m.p.h. ..	17.6 secs.	10.4 secs.
40–60 m.p.h. ..	23.3 secs.	—

ACCELERATION TIMES Through Gears

0–30 m.p.h.	7.4 secs.
0–40 m.p.h.	11.4 secs.
0–50 m.p.h.	17.9 secs.
0–60 m.p.h.	28.3 secs.
Standing quarter-mile ..	25.2 secs.

MAXIMUM SPEED, Flying Quarter-mile

Mean of four opposite runs ..	72.2 m.p.h.
Best time equals	76.9 m.p.h.

BRAKES at 30 m.p.h.

0.68 g. (=44 ft. stopping distance) with 170 lb. pedal pressure.
0.47 g. (=64 ft. stopping distance) with 100 lb. pedal pressure.
0.33 g. (=91 ft. stopping distance) with 50 lb. pedal pressure.

FUEL CONSUMPTION

Overall consumption for 88 miles, 4 gallons—equals 22 m.p.g.
26.5 m.p.g. at constant 30 m.p.h.
24.5 m.p.g. at constant 40 m.p.h.
23.0 m.p.g. at constant 50 m.p.h.
19.5 m.p.g. at constant 60 m.p.h.

HILL CLIMBING

Max. top-gear speed on 1 in 20 .. 48 m.p.h.
Max. top-gear speed on 1 in 15 .. 38 m.p.h.

STEERING

Left-hand lock .. .. .. 41 ft.
Right-hand lock.. .. .. 41 ft.
2¾ turns of steering wheel lock to lock.

Maintenance

Fuel tank : 14 gallons (including 1½ gallons reserve). **Sump :** 11 pints. **Gearbox :** 5 pints. **Fluid flywheel :** 8½ pints. **Rear axle :** 4 pints. **Radiator :** 3¼ gallons. **Firing order :** 1, 5, 3, 6, 2, 4. **Chassis lubrication :** Luvax automatic. **Front wheel toe-in :** ⅛ in. to ³/₁₆ in. **Castor angle :** 1½ degrees. **Camber angle :** 1½ degrees. **King-pin angle :** 5 degrees. **Wheel offset :** 1 2 ins. **Damper fluid :** Luvax piston type. **Tyre pressure :** 28 lb. front, 30 lb. rear. **Lights :** Head-lamp bulbs, 12-volt, 36-watt ; side and tail lamp bulbs, 12-volt, 6-watt ; pass lamp bulb, 12-volt, 60-watt ; stop and reverse lamp bulbs, 12-volt, 24-watt. **Battery :** Lucas 12-volt 69-amp./hr., type SLTW13A.

Ref. No. B/26/47

A30

ADDITION to the 2½-litre Daimler range is this new Consort saloon, which supplements the standard saloon model. It is mounted on a chassis incorporating a number of detail modifications.

DAIMLER MODELS FOR 1950

2½-litre Range Amplified by Additional Saloon on Modified Chassis. Larger Models Mechanically Unchanged

CHIEF innovation in the Daimler range for 1950 is a new saloon, at present for export only, on a modified edition of the 2½-litre chassis. This model, which is known as the Consort, is in addition to the existing saloon model (now distinguished by the title standard saloon) which is continued on the normal chassis. Also continued without change are the 2½-litre drop-head coupe and the 2½-litre Special Sports by Barkers.

Mechanically, the larger cars are unaltered and both the 27 h.p. and Straight Eight chassis continue to be featured with a variety of outstandingly fine coachwork by such renowned builders as Hooper, Windover, Barker and Freestone and Webb. Most of these body styles remain as for 1949, but the four-light and six-light, eight-passenger limousines by Hooper have been replaced by a new eight-passenger limousine styled on the more modern lines of the close-coupled touring limousine by the same coachbuilder.

All these cars are remarkable for the fact that, not only are they fitted with coachwork of the most luxurious and roomy order, but possess a road performance in which refinement is coupled with a maximum speed in the 80 m.p.h. class.

New Model Features

To revert to the 2½-litre range, the new Mulliner-built Consort saloon has the distinctive frontal treatment now familiar on the Special Sports, with the radiator grille swept back in an attractive curve and flanked by head lamps faired into the wings. In general form, the body itself is not unlike that of the standard saloon, except for a more pronounced sweep of the tail; further external points of difference lie in the use of disc, instead of spoked, wheels and the elimination of a sliding roof and opening windscreen, the absence of the latter being compensated for by the fitting of hinged ventilating panels on the front doors.

The body is of the four-six-seater type but the advantages of separate adjustment are retained in the front by the use of close-up seats, which can be lined up when it is desired to carry three abreast. Armrests are provided on the doors and driver-comfort is aided by an adjustable steering column and a seat which can be altered in height as well as reach.

At the rear, the seat is of the usual bench type with a folding centre armrest, but the foundations of the seats are fuller and the upholstery has a new style of pleating. As at the front, the internal dimensions are approximately the same as those of the standard saloon; as with the latter, too, increased internal width is obtained in relation to overall size by the clever expedient of fitting curved thin-framed windows which, by conforming to the curvature of the panelling, reduce the door thickness necessary to accommodate the window in its lowered position.

At the rear, the general arrangement of separate luggage boot and spare-wheel compartments is similar to the standard body, but a difference is found in the use of a bolt-on number plate to avoid the complications which arise abroad with the built-in type.

In general layout, the chassis used for this new Consort saloon follows the familiar 2½-litre specification but with a number of detail, but important changes. The well-known Daimler transmission incorporating a fluid flywheel and preselector epicyclic gearbox is retained (as on all Daimler models), but a hypoid bevel rear axle has been substituted for the underslung worm of the normal chassis, and the ratio is slightly higher, giving overall gearing of 4.3, 6.7, 9.95 and 17.55 to 1.

The six-cylinder engine remains as on the standard chassis except for a change in the pistons (now fitted with three compression rings—two plain and one tapered—and a slotted scraper), while other changes on the mechanical side consist of the use of Girling hydro-mechanical brakes (instead of the purely mechanical type) and the fitting of wider-base rims (5 ins. instead of 4 ins.) for the 6.00 by 16-in. tyres. Owing to the modification of the tail contours and the fitting of a new design of bumper with valance, there is a slight increase in overall length (from 15 ft. to 15 ft. 1½ ins.) whilst the turning circle is 1 ft. greater at 42 ft. In other respects, the two chassis are identical.

EXAMPLE of the luxurious coachwork available on the 27 h.p. and Straight Eight Daimler chassis is this imposing limousine by Freestone and Webb.

BY APPOINTMENT
Motor Car Manufacturers
To the late King George VI

You could hardly hope to find

a car that combines so many points of

excellence, for the man or the

firm with a position to keep up,

as the Daimler Consort

'A most satisfying car, the attraction of which—like the appeal of all good things—grows with acquaintance. . . . in few cars has the journey been done more quickly and in none with such lack of fatigue. . . . designed and built by men who have more of the automobile engineer in their make-up than the production engineer.'—'The Motor' Road Test.

It's undoubtedly a Daimler

THE DAIMLER COMPANY LIMITED, COVENTRY

D94

The Autocar ROAD TESTS

DATA FOR THE DRIVER

2½-LITRE DAIMLER

PRICE, with Consort four-door saloon body, £1,270, plus £353 10s 7d British purchase tax. Total (in Great Britain), £1,623 10s 7d.

ENGINE: 18.02 h.p. (R.A.C. rating), 6 cylinders, overhead valves, 69.6 × 110.49 mm, 2,522 c.c. Brake Horse-power: 70 at 4,200 r.p.m. Compression Ratio: 7 to 1. Max. Torque: 110 lb ft at 2,000 r.p.m. 18.3 m.p.h. per 1,000 r.p.m. on top gear.

WEIGHT: 31 cwt 1 qr 20 lb (3,520 lb). LB. per C.C.: 1.40. B.H.P. per Ton: 44.54.

TYRE SIZE: 6.00 × 16in on bolt-on steel disc wheels.

TANK CAPACITY: 14 English gallons (1½ gallons in reserve). Approximate fuel consumption range, 17–20 m.p.g. (16.6–14.1 litres per 100 km).

TURNING CIRCLE: 42ft 0in (L and R). Steering wheel movement from lock to lock: 3¼ turns. LIGHTING SET: 12-volt.

MAIN DIMENSIONS: Wheelbase, 9ft 6in. Track, 4ft. 4in (front and rear). Overall length, 15ft 2in; width, 5ft 4½in; height, 5ft 5in. Minimum Ground Clearance: 6in.

ACCELERATION

Overall gear ratios	From steady m.p.h. of 10–30 sec	20–40 sec	30–50 sec
4.30 to 1	11.9	13.0	15.7
6.708 to 1	8.1	8.7	11.6
9.976 to 1	6.4	—	—
17.54 to 1	—	—	—

From rest through gears to :—

	sec		sec
30 m.p.h.	8.1	60 m.p.h.	30.1
50 m.p.h.	19.2		

SPEEDS ON GEARS :

(by Electric Speedometer)	M.p.h. (normal and max)	K.p.h. (normal and max)
1st	12—19	19.3—30.6
2nd	25—37	40.2—59.5
3rd	38—54	61.1—86.9
Top	76/77	122/124

Speedometer correction by Electric Speedometer ;—

Car Speedometer m.p.h.	Electric Speedometer m.p.h.
10 =	11.5
20 =	21.0
30 =	30.5
40 =	39.0
50 =	46.5
60 =	56.0
70 =	65.5
80 =	73.5

WEATHER : Dry, warm ; fresh wind.

Acceleration figures are the means of several runs in opposite directions.

Described in " The Autocar " of September 9, 1949.

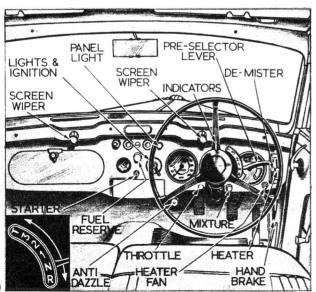

Unmistakably a Daimler, yet modernized, the 2½-litre Consort saloon is a car of quietly distinguished appearance. The thin chromium-plated frames used for the windows permit maximum glass area, resulting in a good outward view for all passengers.

No. 1409 . . . . 2½-LITRE
DAIMLER CONSORT SALOON

FOR the sterling qualities it exhibits, most of them well known to connoisseurs as inherent in the Daimler character, this latest 2½-litre Consort saloon is quickly liked. A comprehensive test, and "living with" the car for a period under owner conditions—which is one of the objects of these Road Tests quite distinct from the application of measuring instruments—leave also an abiding respect for a sound, unspectacular car of high worth. It is sober but distinguished in appearance, it has a roomy five-six-seater body which is comfortable and spacious and also gives the occupants a good view outwards. It is of a size overall that makes it quietly impressive and yet it avoids being unwieldy in the congested traffic of towns, and is used without qualms in narrow roads. It does well just those things that most motorists require of a car. Quality without ostentation is strongly suggested by this car, and it has all the performance ordinary motorists require, plus the ability to carry a full load, up to six people, without apparently making any difference to the handling or performance.

The Consort saloon was newly introduced at the last London Show, principally for export, and offers more spacious coachwork on the well-proved 2½-litre chassis than was provided by the existing model. The main mechanical features are a six-cylinder overhead valve engine in conjunction with the famous fluid flywheel transmission, a pre-selector gear box, and hypoid bevel final drive instead of the worm used for many years on Daimlers, and independent front suspension by means of coil springs. Total weight is lower than might be expected with a body generous in all dimensions, and acceleration is useful, the car quickly getting up to a cruising gait of between 50 and 60 m.p.h. on the open road, and proving lively if the driver wants to handle it briskly. That it is in no sense a dull car is the point that is being stressed; but, conversely, through the special properties with which it is endowed by the hydraulic transmission it is specially suitable to quiet, peaceable driving and pottering round the by-ways. Its suspension shows up well, too, over poor surfaces.

The presence of the fluid flywheel gives almost infinite top gear performance down to zero speed. It is possible to start the Daimler smoothly from rest on top gear, although naturally the acceleration is not then swift, nor would this be a recommended regular procedure. The comment is intended as an illustration of the exceptional ease with which this car can be handled.

No car is easier to drive, since starting from rest is a matter only of engaging first or second gear by moving the lever mounted on the steering column to the appropriate position on its visual quadrant, depressing the gear-changing pedal, which takes the place of a normal clutch

The familiar fluting of the Daimler radiator is preserved in a style similar to that used for the Special Sports; the actual filler cap is under the bonnet.

The body style is conventional and shapely, with wings still sharply defined, and no running boards. The fuel filler cap, seen in the left rear wing, is of locking type.

ROAD TEST
— continued —

pedal, and then depressing the throttle pedal to move away. Subsequent gear changing is carried out similarly, without risk of making a noise, and top and third gears serve for almost all normal driving. Second gear remains in reserve as practically an emergency ratio on which, fully laden, the car will climb a hill of 1 in 6 calibre (approximately 16 per cent).

There is a further decided practical advantage in this transmission in that use of the hand brake for holding the car temporarily on an up gradient is avoided. Suppose that the Daimler is required to wait at traffic lights on such a gradient, circumstances in which many drivers find some difficulty, and when in any case many modern hand brakes prove inconvenient: All that is necessary is to have second gear engaged and to keep the engine gently running, sufficiently to hold the car against gravity on the slope but not fast enough to make it move forward. The left foot remains idle. When the traffic gets away the Daimler moves off smoothly on depression of the throttle pedal. In this particular box the epicyclic gears were not inaudible.

On a journey this car swings along very satisfactorily at 60 plus, and up to a full 70 m.p.h., which is not by any means the maximum, the running is free from suggestion that the engine is being forced. It is found that good times are achieved on a journey without the driver making a special effort to hurry, and that it is a restful car, psychologically as well as physically, to the driver and passengers. The handling qualities are good, and there is a very strong impression of safety about the behaviour at all times.

Suspension characteristics are firm rather than soft. Shocks from road surface deteriorations are absorbed well, though at times there is some vertical movement, strictly limited in its degree. Laterally the car is extremely steady, with the result that, although the owner may never wish to indulge in such methods, it can be taken round bends fast without swaying or any feeling of insecurity. This has the valuable and perhaps more practical corollary, by average standards, that a quick swerve necessitated by an emergency can be safely performed, for in addition the steering is fairly high geared and, therefore, quick. It is reasonably light steering, however, at low speeds and for manœuvring, and at speed feels safe and definite, not calling for any special concentration to keep the car on a normal course. There is nice castor action, the steering wheel coming back positively after taking a 90-degree turn, without the return movement being aggressive. No road shocks worthy of note are transmitted from the road wheels.

An all-but flat floor in the rear compartment and considerable leg room make it spacious above the ordinary for a car of the Daimler's overall dimensions. Polished hardwood and grained leather of fine quality are used to excellent effect.

The easily reached adjusting catches of the front seats are seen, also the vertically adjustable elbow rests on the forward doors. The two halves of the front seats can be adjusted individually, but they meet at the centre and thus make it possible to carry three, the floor being clear of controls.

Confidence is quickly gained in the Girling hydro-mechanical brakes, which operate hydraulically on the front wheels and through rod linkage on the rear wheels. The action from normal pedal depression is well graduated, and with firmer application there is all the power that is wanted for various occasions. The hand brake control is of pistol-grip type, placed to the right under the facia board, where it is quite convenient. As in addition the pre-selector gear lever is in the position it has occupied for many years in connection with the Wilson box, that is, on the steering column, there is freedom from restriction in the front compartment, enabling three to occupy the front seat on occasion. To this end the cushions and back rests meet at the centre, although each section is individually adjustable—an ideal arrangement.

The driving position is comfortable, with plenty of leg room and a large diameter spring-spoked steering wheel which permits considerable latitude according to taste and stature, since it is telescopically adjustable on the column. All the pedal actions have about the same feel and the throttle pedal is a comfortable treadle type. Vision over the bonnet is good. The right-hand wing is fully visible (in a right-hand drive car) and the left wing is in view by leaning over from a normal driving position. In some circumstances the windscreen pillars are rather noticeably wide. A very good view is given by the driving mirror.

Reserve Petrol Supply

The instruments are sensibly arranged and very well illuminated at night, though not too brightly, and there are one or two unusual provisions of value among the minor controls. One of these is a pull-and-push control giving a reserve petrol supply of approximately 1½ gallons, a now most unusual feature which saves many a *contretemps* or need for special thought regarding fuel replenishment; while in addition to a mixture control for cold starting there is a hand throttle. The engine fires at once from cold with very little use of the mixture control, and then with the hand throttle partly opened the car can be, if necessary, reversed out of a garage under the control of the brake pedal.

In the left of the facia is a lockable cupboard. Effective and tasteful use is made of polished hardwood in the body,

Fair luggage space is provided and the interior of the compartment is well finished. The lid can be firmly secured in the open position as a supplementary platform. The lid of the separate compartment in which the spare wheel and tools are carried can be locked by the one key which serves all purposes.

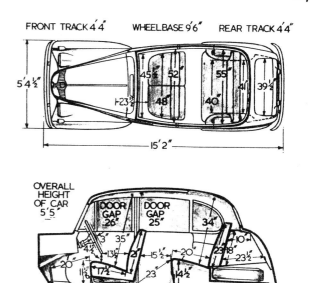

FRONT TRACK 4'4"   WHEELBASE 9'6"   REAR TRACK 4'4"

OVERALL HEIGHT OF CAR 5'5"

SEAT ADJUSTMENT   REAR AXLE

Measurements in these scale body diagrams are taken with the driving seat in the central position of fore and aft adjustment and with the seat cushions uncompressed

which in conjunction with the fine quality grained leather upholstery gives an unmistakable touch of quality, superimposed on the very real quality which is built in beneath the surface of a Daimler. Extended experience of this car, as gained during the present test, produces a strong impression of dependability.

The rear compartment is notably roomy and has a central folding arm rest in the seat back rest. Extra control over ventilation is given by means of pivoted sections in the forward doors, additional to the drop windows. These ventilators can be opened to admit a gentle breeze or be swung round to act as air scoops and promote a really useful cooling draught in hot weather. A sliding roof is not fitted, nor is there a rear window blind.

A heating and windscreen de-icing and demisting system is fitted as standard and controls for this installation are immediately in front of the driver. Fresh air is admitted via this system through a rearward-facing fixed vent, protected by a close mesh, mounted externally on the scuttle.

The horn note is strong, but not unmelodious. On this model the bonnet opens in two sections of upper panel from a central hinge, the release catches being on each side in the front compartment. An excellent feature of the equipment which should contribute materially to chassis longevity, as well as keeping down maintenance charges, is a system of automatic chassis lubrication which takes in all the steering connections and the rear spring shackle pins. This Girling Bijur installation is operated thermally from an expansion chamber in contact with the exhaust manifold. Easily operated D.W.S. jacks, permanently attached, are also part of the equipment.

The two bonnet upper panels are released from inside the car. They give adequate top access to the well-placed auxiliaries, including ignition distributor and carburettor on the left and right sides respectively. The sparking plugs are concealed by a very easily removed moulded plastic cover. Oil and water fillers and the engine dipstick are convenient. Water connections for the interior heater are seen, also the radiator and fan unit mounted neatly on the bulkhead and the air intake vent, on top of the scuttle, for this system. Under-bonnet layout is markedly neat and sensible.

2½-litre DB18 Barker Special Sports, DHC, introduced at 1948 Motor Show. Approx 500 produced 1949-1952.

Same car, which was the prototype, chassis No. 53750. Experts note changes made in the production models.

.he DAIMLER 2½-litre Special Sports Coupé

A medium-sized fast touring car in the grand manner

THE performance figures for the Daimler 2½-litre Coupé which appear on the opposite page represent the truth and nothing but the truth. They singularly fail, however, even to hint at the whole truth concerning the character of what an all-too-brief test in England, France and Belgium showed to be one of the most charming of modern cars.

responsible for designing and making Royal cars have produced in this medium-sized model a car of almost unique character. There are all the most modern refinements of suspension, transmission, and the like, but yet the car retains the individual charm of the handsome, easy running touring cars of a past age.

Unostentatiously finished in dual shades of grey, and proudly carrying a fluted Daimler radiator devoid of name or mock-heraldry, the Barker drop-head body is outstandingly handsome, exploiting to the full the opportunity provided by a chassis of unusually graceful proportions. Inconspicuously as it may travel, the car nevertheless attracts unceasing favourable comment from passers-by, comment which mechanical silence renders almost embarrassingly audible to driver and passengers. If the quality of finish occasionally falls just short of the best standards of traditional craftsmanship, interior and exterior detail work is nevertheless far above the standards of today.

The reason why this model should be designated "sports" frankly escapes us. Granted that it has speed in excess of 80 m.p.h. plus excellent road holding and cornering qualities, it is nevertheless essentially a smooth and inconspicuously fast touring car rather than a vivid sporting one.

Balanced Excellence

The standard of smoothness set is, in every respect, very high indeed. The engine can be felt only when it is idling, and is also inaudible unless exceptionally high r.p.m. are used in the lower gears. The Daimler transmission represents in this instance a fluid flywheel and pre-selective gear box perfectly matched to engine power and car weight. The suspension system maintains riding comfort over a wide range of car speeds and road surfaces. The whole essence of the car is that no single shortcoming mars the overall standard of excellence.

The performance provided by the Daimler lines up with what would be expected from an efficient 2½-litre engine working on unusually high gear ratios to propel a car of good shape, but of luxuriously unstinted weight. There is quite a high maximum speed, almost 85 m.p.h. attained on 85 b.h.p.: there is good fuel economy, more than 30 m.p.g. being attainable when necessary : acceleration, however, is only average for an 18 h.p. car from a standstill up to 50 m.p.h., well maintained up to 70 m.p.h.

ACCESSIBLE MOUNTING.—In view of the special demands of long-distance touring the spare wheel is mounted with fully adequate space around it and is disclosed by swinging clear a large section of the rear panel. The dimensions of the luggage locker above the wheel can also be clearly seen in this photograph.

In assessing the merits of modestly-priced cars, it is of primary importance to record their actual capabilities. Where a car of high quality is concerned, however, performance figures are to be regarded as merely confirming that the car is fast and economical enough for a particular job, the important criterion of value being the degree of refinement and durability, which is offered in comparison with the standards set by cheaper vehicles of perhaps equal speed.

It is fair to say that the engineers

ATTRACTIVE COMPROMISE: The free flowing lines of the Daimler coupé are allied, as shown here, with the traditional form of the high grade British carriage.

25

CLEAR COCKPIT —Attractive lay-out of the front seats and facia panel with pre-selector gear lever mounted on the steering column are well shown in the adjacent photograph

Daimler Road Test - Contd.

and more if required, but relatively gentle, if the overdrive top gear ratio is kept in use down to town speeds.

The primary component of the transmission is the fluid flywheel, a completely smooth form of fluid clutch which gives a smooth start at any time, briskly in first gear or more gently, but quite unprotestingly, in any higher gear even including overdrive top. The secondary transmission unit is an epicyclic gearbox having unusually spaced ratios, 1st and 2nd gears giving 23 m.p.h. and 49 m.p.h. at the engine's maximum power r.p.m., 3rd gear being a direct drive giving 70 m.p.h. at the same engine speed, and top gear being an overdrive on which 101 m.p.h. would have to be attained before the engine would turn at 4,200 r.p.m.

Selection of the ratio to be used at any time is entirely a matter for the driver, no automatic control usurping this privilege. Engagement of any ratio pre-selected by the quadrant control behind the steering wheel, however, takes place smoothly in response to a "kick-down" motion of the left hand of the car's three pedals.

Silent Travel

Until a newcomer becomes familiar with the car, the wide ranges of speed over which the lower gears may be used are not appreciated, but in fact a start from rest in 2nd gear, followed by upward changes at 25 m.p.h. and 38 m.p.h., will only take the rev. counter on the facia panel half-way towards its red maximum indication at 4,500 r.p.m. and will scarcely render the engine audible. Although 3rd gear (being a direct ratio) is perfectly silent, and is perhaps the best traffic ratio, it is perfectly normal practice to use overdrive 4th in town, keeping a lower ratio pre-selected for instant kick-down engagement should quick acceleration be wanted. In days of high-priced fuel this use of overdrive down to low speeds is a sensibly frugal practice for using 3rd gear reduced somewhat surprisingly measured m.p.g. by from 3½ to 6 over the 30-50 m.p.h. range of speeds.

The character of the Daimler is indicated by comparing its performance figures with those of a popular-priced 1950 British saloon, identical in rating of 18 h.p. and noted for high performance. Using a fierce clutch start in place of the smooth fluid flywheel take-off of the Daimler, the popular car can attain 30 m.p.h. in 1½ seconds less time, but is no quicker between 30 and 50 m.p.h., is 2 seconds slower from 50 to 70 m.p.h., and has a maximum speed which the

Daimler driver can match without needing to change into top gear. As an incidental detail, the Daimler has substantially the same fuel consumption as the much lighter quantity-produced steel saloon.

Road driving confirms these figures, for in the confined quarters of busy roads near town the Daimler merely keeps step with the fastest normal traffic, but when the country is reached it strides ahead without fuss or regard for long hills.

Chassis characteristics match the power unit excellently, the car being rarely slowed by road conditions. Although the springing is not of the most extreme softness, it absorbs everything except the worst of bumps encountered at low speeds giving a beautifully steady ride when the car is running at a normal pace.

Quite high geared for a car of substantial weight, the steering is fairly heavy at traffic or parking speeds, but becomes lighter as the speed rises. It gives good feel of the road, without transmitting excessive reaction when Belgian cobblestones are negotiated at 70 m.p.h., combining with the roll-free suspension to make the rapid negotiation of winding roads a pleasure equally for the driver and for his passenger.

As a final touch, the latest Girling braking system ideally matches the velvet gloved character of the car. At any speed, the response to initial pressure on the pedal is gentle, retardation building up

in pleasing progression either to give a satisfactory emergency stop when necessary or to check the car smoothly in any available distance without jerk or tyre howl.

A Road Test Report is not essentially a coachwork review, but details of the Barker body cannot go unmentioned. First, it is quiet, structurally and in regard to wind noise. Secondly, it provides real comfort for 3 or 4 people on its divided bench seat and single rear seat. Thirdly, its hood folds down very completely without threatening to tear, and goes easily into its envelope, leaving an open car which (blessed with an interior heater) can be used pleasurably in very varied weather. Finally, it is well equipped in addition to being handsome.

Smooth Speed

The light-coloured polished wood facia panel carries neat instruments of plain circular form, well calibrated and with variable-brilliance translucent illumination at night. There are cubby holes, door pockets, sun visors, an internal and two external rear-view mirrors, a reserve petrol tap, two separately-switched fog-lamps, and powerful headlamps. The spare wheel and a very complete tool kit are accommodated in a compartment below the luggage locker, of which the lid is spring counterbalanced. Engine accessibility also appears good, despite rather clumsy bonnet-catch arrangements, but in accordance with Daimler practice the battery is rather too well concealed under the floor.

Strikingly good looking, and with a talent for rapid and exceedingly smooth long-distance travel, the Daimler is a car which anyone can appreciate. Responding also to intelligent handling of the controls by giving the ultimate in smoothly quick progress, it is a simple-to-drive car which, nevertheless, has a very special appeal for the keen driver.

ALTERNATIVE SEATING: Although it is possible to carry three persons on the front seat the aft-mounted transverse seat will be found particularly useful for long distances. With two persons carrying a large amount of luggage the seat can be removed and the whole rear space made available for suitcases, etc.

The **Motor** Continental Road Test No. 6C/50

Make: Daimler　　　　**Type:** 2½-litre Special Sports Coupe

Makers: The Daimler Co., Ltd., Coventry

Dimensions and Seating

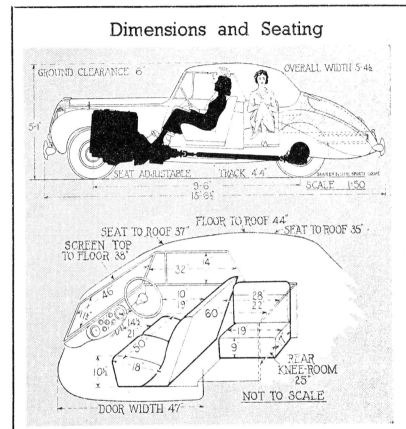

GROUND CLEARANCE 6"　　OVERALL WIDTH 5-4½

5-1"

SEAT ADJUSTABLE　　TRACK 4-4"　　SCALE 1:50

9-6½
15-6½

FLOOR TO ROOF 44"
SEAT TO ROOF 37"　　SEAT TO ROOF 35"
SCREEN TOP TO FLOOR 38"

REAR KNEE-ROOM 25"

NOT TO SCALE

DOOR WIDTH 47"

In Brief

Price £1,645, plus purchase tax, £457 13 11 equals £2,102 13 11.
Capacity .. .. .. 2,522 c.c.
Unladen kerb weight .. 32½ cwt.
Fuel consumption .. .. 23.1 m.p.g.
Maximum speed .. .. 84.1 m.p.h.
Maximum speed on 1 in 20 gradient.. .. 52-66 m.p.h.
Maximum direct gear gradient 1 in 10.3
Maximum overdrive gradient 1 in 14.9
Acceleration,
　10-30 m.p.h. in top. 9.8—14.4 secs.
　0.50 m.p.h. through gears. 16.1 secs.
Gearing,
　22.7 m.p.h. in overdrive top at 1,000 r.p.m.
　78 m.p.h. at 2,500 ft. per min. piston speed.
(Direct 3rd gear figures, 16.6 m.p.h. and 57 m.p.h.).

Specification

Engine
Cylinders 6
Bore .. .. 69.6 mm.
Stroke .. .. .. 110.5 mm.
Cubic Capacity .. .. 2,522 c.c.
Piston area .. .. 35.4 sq. ins.
Valves .. .. .. Pushrod o.h.v.
Compression ratio 7.0/1
Max. power .. .. .. 85 b.h.p.
　at .. .. .. 4,200 r.p.m.
Piston speed at max. b.h.p. 3,050 ft. per min.
Carburetter .. .. Twin S.U. horizontal
Ignition .. .. .. Lucas coil
Sparking plugs .. 14 mm. Lodge CB 14
Fuel pump .. .. .. AC Mechanical
Oil Filter .. .. Tecalemit full flow
Transmission
Clutch .. .. .. Fluid flywheel
Gearbox .. .. .. Pre-selective
Top gear (overdrive) 3.55
3rd gear (direct) 4.857
2nd gear 7.97
1st gear 14.57
Propeller shaft .. .. Hardy Spicer
Final drive .. Underslung worm, 7/34
Chassis
Brakes .. .. Girling hydro-mech.
Brake drum diameter .. .. 11 ins.
Friction lining area .. 146 sq. ins.
Suspension :
　Front .. Coil and wishbone I.F.S.
　Rear .. .. Semi-elliptic
Shock absorbers .. .. Luvax hydraulic
Tyres .. .. 6.00 x 16
Steering
Steering gear　Marles worm and double roller
Turning circle .. .. 42 ft.
Turns of steering wheel, lock to lock .. 2¾
Performance Factors (at laden weight as tested)
Piston area, sq. in. per ton 19.7
Brake lining area, sq. in. per ton .. 81
Specific displacement, litres per ton mile 1,850 in overdrive top, 2,540 in direct 3rd.
Fully described in " The Motor," October 20th, 1948.

Test Conditions

Mild weather, strong side wind, dry concrete surface, Belgian pump fuel. Car tested on Ostend-Ghent motor road.

Test Data

ACCELERATION TIMES on Upper Ratios.

	Overdrive 4th	Direct 3rd	2nd
10-30 m.p.h.	14.4 secs.	9.8 secs.	6.5 secs.
20-40 m.p.h.	14.9 secs.	10.0 secs.	6.7 secs.
30-50 m.p.h.	16.9 secs.	11.2 secs.	9.4 secs.
40-60 m.p.h.	20.2 secs.	12.9 secs.	—
50-70 m.p.h.	26.1 secs.	17.4 secs.	—

MAXIMUM SPEEDS
Flying Quarter Mile
Mean of four opposite runs .. 84.1 m.p.h.
Best time equals .. .. 86.5 m.p.h.

Speed in Gears
(Red mark on tachometer)
Max. speed in 3rd gear .. .. 78 m.p.h.
Max. speed in 2nd gear .. .. 48 m.p.h.

ACCELERATION TIMES Through Gears
0-30 m.p.h. .. .. 7.3 secs.
0-40 m.p.h. .. .. 11.0 secs.
0-50 m.p.h. .. .. 16.1 secs.
0-60 m.p.h. .. .. 23.3 secs.
0-70 m.p.h. .. .. 33.5 secs.
Standing quarter mile .. .. 23.7 secs.

HILL CLIMBING (at steady speeds)
Max. speed on 1 in 20 .. .. 52 m.p.h. in overdrive 4th.
　　　　　　　　　　　　66 m.p.h. in direct 3rd.
Max. speed on 1 in 15 .. .. 30 m.p.h. in overdrive 4th.
　　　　　　　　　　　　60 m.p.h. in direct 3rd.
Max. gradient on 4th gear .. 1 in 14.9 (Tapley 150 lb./ton).
Max. gradient on 3rd gear .. 1 in 10.3 (Tapley 215 lb./ton).
Max. gradient on 2nd gear .. 1 in 6.6 (Tapley 335 lb./ton).

BRAKES at 30 m.p.h.
0.82 g. retardation (=36½ ft. stopping distance) with 120 lb. pedal pressure.
0.74 g. retardation (=40½ ft. stopping distance) with 100 lb. pedal pressure.
0.37 g. retardation (=81 ft. stopping distance) with 50 lb. pedal pressure.

FUEL CONSUMPTION
32.0 m.p.g. at constant 30 m.p.h.
29.5 m.p.g. at constant 40 m.p.h.
26.5 m.p.g. at constant 50 m.p.h.
24.0 m.p.g. at constant 60 m.p.h.
21.5 m.p.g. at constant 70 m.p.h.
Overall consumption for 305 miles, 13.2 gallons, equals 23.1 m.p.g.

WEIGHT
Unladen kerb weight .. .. 32½ cwt.
Front/rear weight distribution .. 51/49
Weight laden as tested .. .. 36 cwt.

INSTRUMENTS
Speedometer at 30 m.p.h. .. 4% slow
Speedometer at 60 m.p.h. .. 4% fast
Speedometer at 90 m.p.h. .. 10% fast
Distance recorder .. .. Accurate

Maintenance

Fuel tank: 14 gallons. Sump: 11 pints, S.A.E. 30 oil. Fluid Flywheel: 8½ pints, S.A.E. 30 oil. Gearbox: 5 pints, S.A.E. 30 oil. Rear Axle: 4 pints. Steering gear: S.A.E. 140 gear oil. Radiator: 26 pints (2 drain taps). Chassis lubrication: Luvax Bijur automatic. Ignition timing: 8° B.T.D.C. Firing Order: 1:5:3:6:2:4. Spark plug gap: 0.020 in. Contact breaker gap: 0.012 in. Valve timing: I.O., 11° B.T.D.C. I.C., 63° A.B.D.C., E.O. 63° B.B.D.C., E.C. 11° A.T.D.C. Tappet clearances: (hot) 0.013 in. Front wheel toe-in: ⅛ in.-⅜ in. Camber angle: 1½°. Castor angle: 1½°. Tyre pressures: Front 28 lb., rear 30 lb. Brake fluid: Girling crimson. Battery: Lucas SLTW 13A, 12-volt 60 amp. hour. Lamp bulbs: Headlamps, Lucas No. 302, 48/48 watt. Sidelamps, Lucas No. 207, 6 watt. Fog lamps, Lucas No. 162, 36 watt. Rear and brake light, Lucas No. 189, 6/24 watt. Rear No. plate, Lucas No. 989, 6 watt. Reverse lamp, Lucas No. 199, 24 watt. Ref. B/26/50.

796

Daimler's Special Sports must be one of the
world's most beautiful cars in its usual drop-
head coupé form, and the saloon top conversion by Appleyard of Leeds, Ltd., blends well
with the graceful lines of the standard model.
The visibility is considerably improved compared with that of the fabric top version.

The De luxe 'Empress' 2½-litre Daimler Saloon with special coachwork by Hooper of London, Exhibited at the New York Show

America admires a British car

DAIMLER

CUSTOM-BUILT FOR THE CONNOISSEUR

BY APPOINTMENT
MOTOR CAR MANUFACTURERS
TO H.M. THE KING

29

CLOSED —The flowing lines of the Hooper Daimler 2½-litre are emphasized by the front wing treatment and sloping radiator-shell. Note the entire suppression of rear wings as such.

LUXURY in DROPHEADS

An Electrically-operated Model by Hooper on Special Series 2½-litre Daimler Chassis

ALL-ELECTRIC—The hood is quickly erected or folded by means of an electric motor. An additional unit raises and lowers the decking over the compartment into which it folds. Note (right) the neat stowage of the hood, and the large luggage boot.

THE "touring-car" as a body style is a thing of the past; but the touring-car, in the sense of a vehicle for fast, luxurious travel over long distances has more to offer today than at any period in history. An instance of this is the drophead body built recently by Hooper & Co. (Coachbuilders) Ltd. to the order of Mr. I. Donelly, of Messrs. P. and D. Developments, on a Special Series 2½-litre Daimler chassis.

The lines are typical of the best English practice; elegant and restrained, they owe nothing to transatlantic fashions, while possessing a dignity and balance of their own. This body recalls in certain particulars the sensational drop-

FULLY APPOINTED—Seating four persons in great comfort, the upholstery is in biscuit-coloured hide, which tones well with the rich figuring of the Australian camphor-wood facia. Normally electrically-operated, the windows may be raised manually, by means of normal winders. Note the sun blinds.

head coupé Straight-eight Daimler exhibited by Hooper and Co. at the Motor Show of 1949. Both cars have a curved, laminated Triplex windscreen with pillars well back, to give a good visibility, and both exhibit a feature which enhances the sweeping lines, namely the total elimination of rear wings.

The machine illustrated is noteworthy also for a number of special features designed in conjunction with Mr. Donelly. Operation of the hood is effected in what must now be regarded as the orthodox fashion for cars of the highest quality: by an electric motor. In addition to the standard P. and D. unit mounted below the rear floorboards, however, the car illustrated has a small ancillary motor behind the squab, the effect of which is to raise and lower the decking which covers the hood when in the open position.

Other ingenious electrical applications are the window-winding and a small motor under the bonnet, actuated by a thermostatically-controlled relay switch, whose function is to raise or lower a roller blind between the radiator core and grille. This not only accelerates the warming-up of the engine, but also brings the heater into operation in a shorter space of time.

Similar Daimler drophead coupés with identical coachwork have been supplied to H.M. The King for his personal use, and to Queen Marie of Roumania.

NEW CARS DESCRIBED

NEW DAIMLER SALOON WITH A PRICE THAT NEEDS NO MNEMONIC

Designed as a four-five-seater saloon, this car has a nicely balanced appearance. The body is virtually a four-light design, with the very good feature of the addition of rear ventilating panels.

ANOTHER 1066 CONQUEST

CARS produced by the Daimler company have a long-standing reputation for quality and detail finish of a very high order; they also have an air of dignity and tradition that fits them for the task of providing Royal transport. The detail work and finish built into a car, do of course, influence the price that must be paid for the finished article. Daimlers are not cheap cars; on the other hand they give the craftsman an opportunity to show the world that Britain can produce quality cars that are second to none, as has been emphasized by examples displayed at the London Show.

Two Daimler cars in particular seen at the past two Shows have been the cause of much comment because of their elaborate finish and detail fittings; they have, in fact, been criticized by some people who

consider that such cars are not practical. This may be so if they are considered as vehicles for everyday use instead of exhibition pieces displaying very fine workmanship. A ball dress by Dior or Hartnell would not be condemned just because it would not be practical on a shopping expedition.

However, the factor of utility is one that the car manufacturer must carefully consider for the cars that provide the bulk of his business and this has been done very effectively in the latest addition to the Daimler range now announced.

This new model, known as the Conquest, is small by Daimler standards, and is designed to cater for the driver who requires a vehicle of high quality and detail finish, coupled with a good performance, but does not want a very large or heavy car.

This new car was designed and brought into production in a period of about four months, a very enterprising effort. Obviously, it would not be possible to design and produce in quantity a car that was completely new in such a short time, as the manufacture of press tools alone would take longer than the time allowed. The solution, then, was to use any existing components that were suitable and so reduce the number of completely new components required—a policy that is very sound, as it makes use of previous development work, reduces cost, and, by the resulting measure of standardization, is an aid to servicing.

The main item that is new in the new Daimler is the engine; this is fitted in a slightly modified version of the Lanchester Leda chassis. The majority of the body

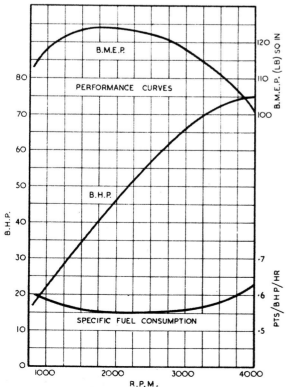

Performance curves of the Conquest engine.

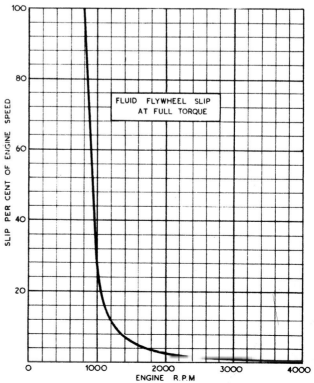

This graph shows the fluid flywheel characteristics.

31

ANOTHER 1066 CONQUEST . . . continued

pressings are also similar to those of the Leda, but the frontal treatment is modified and the car wears the familiar fluted Daimler raditaor grille. The interior trim is completely new and in keeping with the general high quality finish associated with the products of the Daimler company.

The engine, a six-cylinder overhead-valve unit, has a capacity of 2,433 c.c. and develops 75 b.h.p. at 4,000 r.p.m. This results in a power-weight ratio of 53 b.h.p. per ton compared with 40.6 b.h.p. per ton for the Lanchester Leda (running weight is used in both cases). This means that a power unit which develops more power and has two extra cylinders has been accommodated without redesigning the frame, which was originally produced to take a four-cylinder power unit.

There are a number of interesting features about this overhead-valve six-cylinder engine. With cylinder dimensions of 76.2 × 89mm (3 × 3.5in), the bore is of the same diameter as that of both the 2-litre Lanchester Leda and the 3-litre Daimler Regency, but the stroke is considerably shorter, resulting in a bore-stroke ratio of 0.856 to 1. The cast-iron cylinder block and crankchamber is of very stiff construction, and has a clean exterior; it is split on the crankshaft centre line and well ribbed to support the four main

The figuring of the facia panels is particularly pleasing. The instruments include fuel gauge, ammeter, water temperature gauge and clock. A fuel reserve tap and hand throttle are provided.

bearings. All the bores are completely surrounded by water jackets which extend well below the exposed portion when the piston is at the bottom of its stroke. Dry cylinder liners are used and they are fine bored and honed in position. Particular attention is paid to the positioning of the cylinder head stud bosses so that the bores are not distorted when the head is tightened down. The bottom of the crank-

chamber is enclosed by a deep cast, light alloy sump which has a baffle plate in the rear section around the oil pump.

The crankshaft is of massive construction, and, because of the relatively short stroke and large journal diameter, there is a considerable amount of overlap between the main and big-end bearings. Balance weights are placed at the ends of the shaft outside Nos 1 and 6 big-end bearings, and also on the outside of Nos 3 and 4, between the two centre main bearings. It is claimed that this method simplifies the construction of the crank, reduces the overall weight and provides a satisfactory degree of balance. A Metalastik torsional vibration damper is fitted to the front of the crankshaft.

All the four main bearings are 2½in diameter and have a bearing length of 1¼in; conseqently the steel-backed white metal bearings are all interchangeable. Dowels are used to position the main bearing caps, and thrust is taken by two semi-circular thrust washers placed in recesses, one on each side of the front main bearing cap. No thrust washers are fitted to the block. The

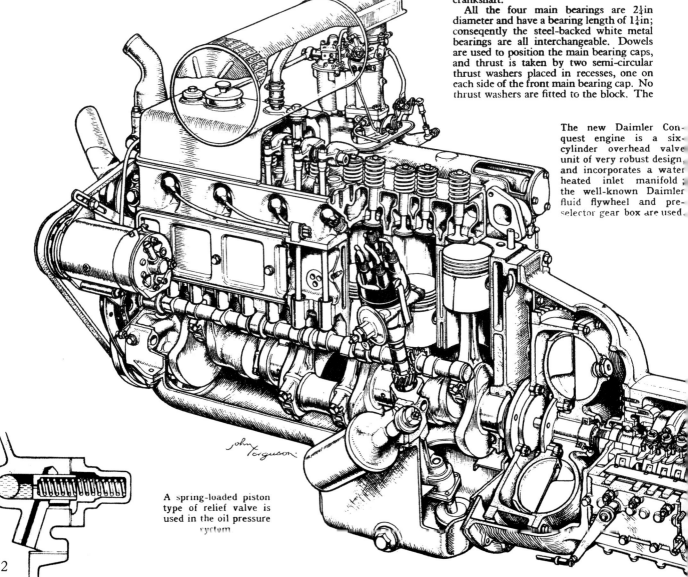

The new Daimler Conquest engine is a six-cylinder overhead valve unit of very robust design, and incorporates a water heated inlet manifold; the well-known Daimler fluid flywheel and pre-selector gear box are used.

A spring-loaded piston type of relief valve is used in the oil pressure system

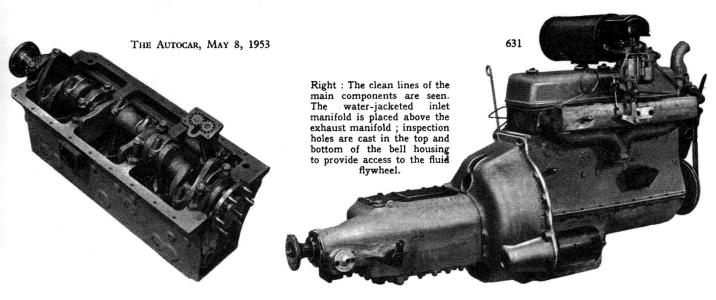

Right : The clean lines of the main components are seen. The water-jacketed inlet manifold is placed above the exhaust manifold ; inspection holes are cast in the top and bottom of the bell housing to provide access to the fluid flywheel.

The crankchamber is divided into three separate compartments by the webs which support the main bearings. The massive proportions of the crankshaft and the disposition of the balance weights can be seen. The oil pump bottom cover is removed to show the gears.

big-end bearings are 2in in diameter and have a bearing length of 1 5/8 in. The H-section connecting rods measure 6 1/2 in between centres; to facilitate assembly they are split on an angle so that the big-end will pass through the cylinder bore. The two parts of the rod are located by tubular dowels and held together by set bolts locked together with tab washers. Like the main bearings, the big-end bearings are of steel-backed white metal.

The camshaft is also supported in four main bearings, and these are again steel-backed white metal. Chilled cast iron is used for the shaft and the cams are of a special design that provides a more uniform acceleration than the normal type; they produce fast valve opening to ensure good breathing. The cam form also helps to reduce spring surge; the valve gear is

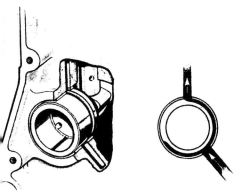

A groove cast in the rear bearing of the camshaft meters oil to the overhead valve gear.

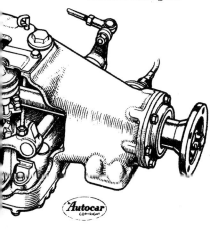

quiet in operation and only one spring per valve is used; circlips are fitted to the stems to prevent a valve falling into the engine in the event of spring failure. To save weight the end of the camshaft is counterbored. The drive is by normal duplex chain. The remainder of the valve gear is conventional, with 7/8 in diameter piston-type tappets (with an escape hole to prevent oil becoming trapped) used with tubular push rods, which have hardened end plugs. Case-hardened rockers pivot direct on the rocker shaft.

The lubrication system is fed by a double gear pump situated low down and towards the rear of the engine, and driven by a spindle geared to the camshaft. This spindle does not pass through the pump delivery duct, but is supported by two bearings, the lower one formed by the pump casing; the upper one is a bush in the crankchamber. Oil from the pump passes through an outlet drilled in the crankcase into the full-flow filter bolted on the left side of the engine. After passing through the filter, which is fitted with a by-pass valve (so that the engine is not starved of oil in the event of the filter becoming blocked), the oil passes through another drilling in the crankcase to the main oil gallery—a 5/8 in diameter hole running the length of the block.

Oil to the overhead valve gear is metered by a cast-in groove running half-way round the rear camshaft journal. This allows an intermittent supply of oil to pass through a drilling in the bearing and block to an internal pipe connected by means of a banjo to the hollow rocker spindle. This is cross-drilled to lubricate the rockers.

The relief valve, consisting of a spring-loaded piston, is set to blow at 40lb per sq in. A warning light operated by a pressure switch is used in place of an oil pressure gauge. This is usual Daimler practice. An interesting feature about the lubrication system, and an indication of the trouble taken by the makers to ensure that their products reach the owner in the best possible condition, is the running-in arrangement. There is a hole in the bottom of the sump just below the pump intake to enable an external oil supply to be piped to the pump intake

when the engine is on the test bed; consequently it is very thoroughly flushed and cleaned during the initial running-in period. This hole is later sealed with a plug that fits flush with the bottom of the sump. The inside of the plug extends up through the sump and forms a shroud to prevent sludge being drawn into the pump intake. A normal type of drain plug is fitted on the side of the sump.

Fourteen 7/16 in diameter studs secure the cylinder head, which has combustion chambers that can best be described as modified " bath tub " shape, with the top face sloping at 7 degrees (thus the valve stems are also set at an angle of 7 degrees to the vertical). There is a small squish area opposite the sparking plug. The flat-top pistons are similar to those used in the Lanchester Leda and Daimler Regency engines. Valve seat inserts are provided on the exhaust ports only and the usual Daimler practice of one port per valve is employed.

Particular attention is paid to the cooling arrangements of the cylinder head. Water from the pump passes into the block, and then to the head via holes in the top face of the block, which connect with slotted thimbles pressed into holes in the cylinder head; these direct the coolant so that it impinges on the valve ports

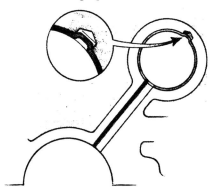

The camshaft bearings are held in place by punching the shell into a dimple which is an extension of the oil hole drilling.

Separate ports are provided for each valve. Thimbles placed in the cylinder head direct the cooling water around the exhaust valve ports.

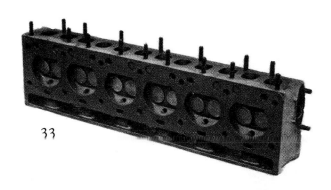

33

ANOTHER 1066 CONQUEST . . . . continued

where it is most needed. On the opposite side of the cylinder head slots allow water to pass from the block round the sparking plug bosses. With the thermostat closed all the coolant passes from the cylinder head into the manifold water jacket and back to the pump. It is claimed that this large flow through the manifold water jacket provides a quick and more efficient heat transfer to the inside of the manifold during the warming up period than could be obtained with an exhaust gas hot-spot system. With the thermostat valve open there is no direct flow through the manifold water jacket, but the water does form an effective means of insulating the inlet manifold from excess exhaust heat.

In conjunction with the new engine the well-known Daimler fluid flywheel is used. This unit, as well as the four-speed pre-selector gear box, is identical with that fitted on the Lanchester Leda. The crankshaft is directly coupled (by means of the casing) to the rear or driving section of the flywheel, a circular aluminium alloy casting containing a number of vanes. The output or driven side of the flywheel is similar in construction to the impellor, but it is placed between the engine and the driving member, and coupled to the input side of the gear box. There are 48 vanes on the driving member, and 45 vanes on the driven member; the difference in number is to ensure quiet operation.

Two filler plugs are fitted in the outer casing of the flywheel so that the unit can be drained and refilled with oil without rotating the crankshaft. It is essential that the correct oil level in the flywheel should be maintained, to ensure that the unit functions efficiently. A graph shows the slip curve at full torque; slip is 100 per cent of engine speed at 800 r.p.m. This means that if the car were stationary, in gear, with the hand brake on and the throttle fully open, the engine speed would not rise above 800

The laminated torsion bars for the independent front suspension are located parallel to, and on the inside of, the frame side members. The telescopic front dampers pass through the upper wishbones.

r.p.m. The curve also shows that in the normal operating range the efficiency of the unit is very high.

From the fluid flywheel the drive is transmitted to the four-speed epicyclic gear box, which is also similar to that used on the Leda. It consists of four gear trains with their respective brake bands to provide the indirect and reverse gear ratios, as well as a lock-up multi-plate clutch to provide a direct drive for top gear. The gears are selected manually by moving the camshaft which is coupled to the steering column gear lever by means of rods and levers; the actual gear engagement is performed by operating the " clutch pedal," which is connected to the bus bar. It is the bus bar spring that applies the load necessary to lock the plate clutch or hold the drums. With different gear ratios the load required to hold the drum will vary; this is compensated for by grooving the outside of the drums, the angle of the grooves being 55 degrees for first and reverse gears and 90 degrees for second and third. Lubrication for the box is by an oscillating pump driven by the input shaft.

Laminated Torsion Bars

The chassis frame has box section side members (perforated on the inner webs to save weight); it has a cruciform bracing as well as four other cross members. The main front cross member is also box section and both the horizontal plates are perforated, again to save weight. Although an orthodox system of rear suspension is used, a somewhat unusual system is employed at the front, consisting of laminated torsion bars. This arrangement has several advantages: with this layout it is much more simple and less costly to arrange the lever and anchorage fixings, as splines do not have to be cut; also it is not necessary to grind the surfaces of the spring blades which form the bar. It is sometimes claimed that the friction between the blades helps to damp the system, but in this application the relative movement (between the blades) is very small.

The springs fit into square holes in the attachment adaptors; these are flnaged for and bolted to the frame or the lower wishbones. A vernier adjustment is provided by drilling 18 holes for the rear adaptor and 20 for the front. A feature that considerably reduces the maintenance cost of the car as well as increasing its life is the chassis lubrication system. Those chassis bearings that are not formed by rubber bushes are lubricated by a system of pipes which supply lubricant from a tank mounted under the bonnet. The system is operated automatically by an expansion chamber situated close to the exhaust pipe; the change in temperature when the engine is cold and hot causes the lubricant to be drawn into the chamber and forced

Lubricant is piped to the suspension bearings from an automatic lubrication system.

out to lubricate the bearings. The only points that require lubrication by a gun are the propeller-shaft, water pump and rear wheel bearings. Grease cups are provided for the front hub bearings.

The Autocar Road Test of the Conquest appears on following pages.

SPECIFICATION

Engine.—6 cyl, 76.2 × 88.9 mm (2,433 c.c.). Compression ratio 6.6 to 1. Four-bearing. Modified " bath-tub " combustion chamber. Side camshaft operating overhead valves by push rods and rockers.

Transmission.—Daimler fluid flywheel and pre-selector gear box, 4 forward speeds. Overall ratios: Top 4.56, third 6.71, second 10.05, first 17.47 to 1; reverse 23.7 to 1.

Final Drive.—Hypoid with four-pinion differential. Ratio 4.56 to 1 (9:41).

Suspension. — Front, independent by laminated torsion bars and wishbones. Girling telescopic dampers, anti-roll bar. Rear, half-elliptic leaf springs, telescopic dampers. Suspension rate (at the wheel): front 85 lb per in; rear 114 lb per in.

Brakes.—Girling Hydro-mechanical, two-leading shoe front. Drum diameter, 11in front and rear. Drum width 1⅜in front and rear. Total lining area front and rear, 70.5 sq in.

Steering.—Bishop cam (cam and roller); 18 to 1 ratio at gear.

Wheels and Tyres.—Dunlop 6.70-15in on 5-stud steel disc wheels.

Electrical Equipment.—12-volt; 51 ampère-hour battery. Head lamps: double-dip, 42-36 watt bulbs.

Fuel System.—15-gallon tank. Oil capacity 10 pints. Tecalemit full-flow filter.

Main Dimensions.—Wheelbase 8ft 8in. Track (front), 4ft 4in; (rear), 4ft 4in. Overall length 14ft 9½in. Width 5ft 6in. Height, running trim, 5ft 5in. Ground clearance 7in. Turning circle 34ft. Weight (in running trim with 15 gallons fuel) 28½ cwt.

Price.—£1,066; purchase tax in Great Britain £445 5s 10d. Total (in Great Britain), £1,511 5s 10d.

The main frame side members are of block section with perforated channel section cruciform cross braces.

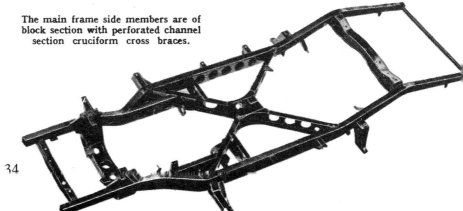

THE CONQUEST
—A New 2½-litre Daimler

New Six-cylinder Model of More Compact Size and Lower Weight Powered by Short-stroke Engine Developing 75 b.h.p.

ANY new model from the old-established Daimler company constitutes an event of considerable note. The new 2½-litre Daimler Conquest, which is being publicly announced today, will command widespread attention for the way in which traditions established in the earliest days have been blended with current ideas and requirements.

In appearance, the Conquest is typically Daimler in the more recent post-war style; in size, it is 5 in. shorter than the 2½-litre Consort—which it supersedes—and gives four/five-seater accommodation more compactly arranged; in weight, it is over 3 cwt. lighter than its forerunner; in power, it offers an additional 5 b.h.p. (at lower peak r.p.m.); and in basic price it is nearly £140 cheaper even than the latest price of the Consort, the Conquest costing £1,066, plus £445 5s. 10d. tax—a total of £1,511 5s. 10d.

In short, this new 2½-litre Conquest model is designed for the business, professional or family user who requires a car of medium size, very lively performance and more-than-ordinary refinement, but who, nevertheless, cannot afford to ignore the cost factor entirely. Notable design points include an entirely new six-cylinder engine of the short-stroke type, a robust chassis with indepedent front suspension by means of laminated torsion bars, a pressed-steel body furnished to typical Daimler standards and the well-known Daimler transmission incorporating a fluid flywheel and pre-selector gearbox.

Elsewhere in this issue we publish a Road Test Report on this notable new model.

*   *   *

Of straightforward design with push-rod-operated overhead valves, the six-cylinder engine represents a breakaway from the long-stroke Daimler tradition, the Conquest having a bore/stroke ratio of 1/1.17, compared with the 1/1.59 of the Consort and the 1/1.42 of the more-recently-designed 3-litre Regency type. In adopting this near-square ratio, the chief engineer, Mr. C. M. Simpson has taken into account not only the advantages of short-stroke engines in reduced piston speeds, but also the increasing difficulties in obtaining good combustion shape with present-day compression ratios as the bore/stroke ratio approaches unity; the chosen dimensions (76.2 mm. by 88.9 mm.) are regarded as representing a good compromise between these conflicting advantages.

In-line overhead valves are inclined at 7° to the vertical (compared with 10° on the Consort), with the inlets of larger diameter ($1\frac{7}{16}$ in.) than the exhausts ($1\frac{5}{16}$ in.). Detail points of interest are that the heads of the exhausts are of greater thickness in the interests of good heat absorption and that their stems are copper plated, both to reduce sticking tendencies and to assist in heat dissipation, whilst inserted seats of Bromachrome are used.

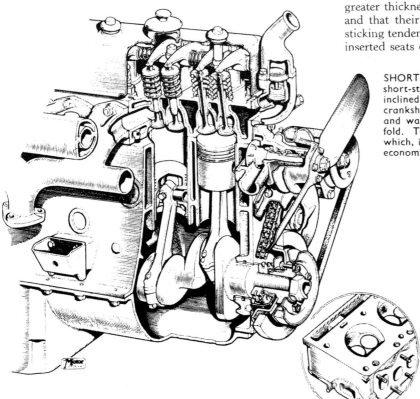

SHORT STROKE. This broken-open drawing of the new short-stroke 2½-litre Daimler Conquest engine reveals the inclined valves, dry cylinder liners, massive counter-balanced crankshaft, Metalastik torsional vibration damper, camshaft and water-pump drive, and water-heated induction manifold. The inset drawing shows the cylinder head shape, which, in conjunction with the porting, gives the excellent economy, power output and low-speed torque characteristics shown by the graph below.

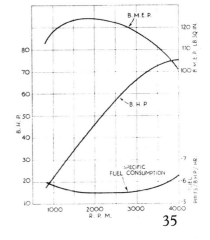

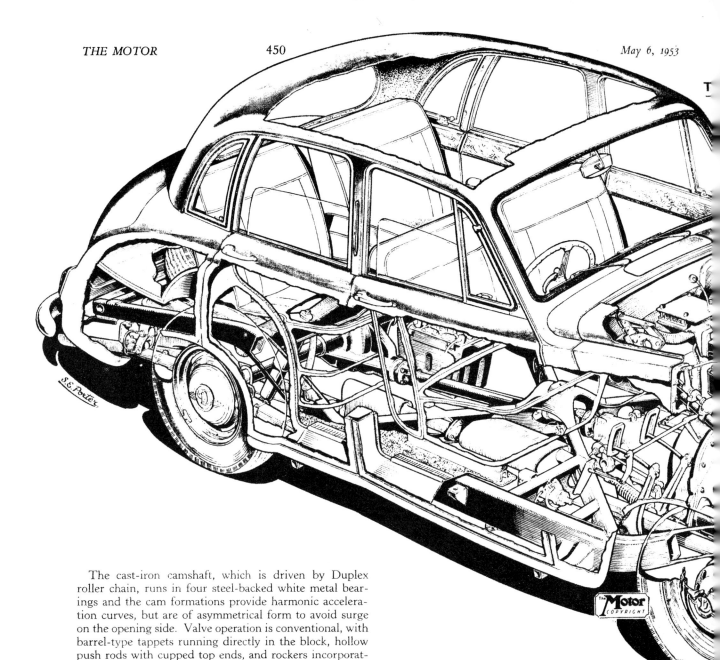

The cast-iron camshaft, which is driven by Duplex roller chain, runs in four steel-backed white metal bearings and the cam formations provide harmonic acceleration curves, but are of asymmetrical form to avoid surge on the opening side. Valve operation is conventional, with barrel-type tappets running directly in the block, hollow push rods with cupped top ends, and rockers incorporating the usual ball ended adjuster; single springs of large diameter (which are used primarily to reduce stresses but also serve to keep down the overall height of the engine) are used, and are retained by split cotters.

Engine Refinements

The combustion chambers are lozenge-shaped, the flat portion of the head over-lapping the bore on one side to provide a "squish" turbulence effect as the piston approaches the top of its stroke. The long-reach 14 mm. sparking plugs, inserted at an angle at one side of the head, are symmetrically placed in relation to the valve heads.

Special attention has been paid to obtaining good gas flow, both by careful valve positioning and by port layout, and an interesting point in the latter connection is that the lower ends of the exhaust valve guides are almost flush with the port walls, so causing little obstruction as well as providing maximum cooling of the guide. The inlet manifold, cast in DTD 424 aluminium alloy and anodized to prevent corrosion, is notable for two points, both of which follow the practice adopted on the 3-litre Regency engine. One is the use of separate porting to each cylinder (considered desirable in view of the larger valve overlap period of 39°) and the other is the fact that, instead of the more common hot-spot arrangement, the manifold is water-jacketted throughout; this jacket, in fact, constitutes the thermostat by-pass circuit, water from the pump entering

36

DAIMLER CONQUEST DATA

Engine Dimensions			Transmission (Contd.)		
Cylinders	6		Gear ratios: 1st ...		
Bore	76.2 mm.		Rev. ...		
Stroke	88.9 mm.		Prop. shaft		Har
Cubic capacity ...	2,433 c.c.		Final drive		
Piston area	42.4 sq. in.		**Chassis Details**		
Valves	Overhead (push rod)		Brakes		Girli
Compression ratio ...	6.6				ical
Engine performance			Brake drum diameter		
Max. power ...	75 b.h.p.		Friction lining area		
at	4,000 r.p.m.		Suspension: Front ...		Inde
Max. b.m.e.p. ...	124 lb./sq. in.				ated
at	1,600 r.p.m.		Rear ...		
B.H.P. per sq. in			Shock absorbers ...		Teles
piston area	1.77		Wheel type ...		
Peak piston speed ft.			Tyre size		
per min.	2,330		Steering gear ...		
Engine Details			Steering wheel ...		17-ir
Carburetter... ...	Zenith downdraught		**Dimensions**		
	42VIS		Wheelbase		
Ignition	Coil		Track: Front and rear		
Plugs: make and type	Lodge CLN		Overall length ...		
Fuel pump	AC Mechanical		Overall width ...		
Fuel capacity ...	15 gallons		Overall height ...		
Oil filter (make, by-			Ground clearance ...		
pass or full flow)...	Tecalemit full-flow		Turning circle ...		
Oil capacity ...	10 pints		Dry weight		
Cooling system ...	Pump, fan and thermo-		**Performance Data**		
	stat		Piston area, sq. in		
Water capacity ...	19 pints		per ton		
Electrical system ...	12-volt Lucas		Brake lining area,		
Battery capacity ...	51 amp./hr.		sq. in per ton ...		
			Top gear m.p.h. per		
Transmission			1,000 r.p.m. ...		
Clutch	Daimler fluid flywheel		Top gear m.p.h. at		
	and pre-selector trans-		2,500 ft./min. piston		
	mission		speed		
Gear ratios: Top ...	4.56		Litres per ton-mile,		
3rd ...	6.71		dry		
2nd ...	10.05				

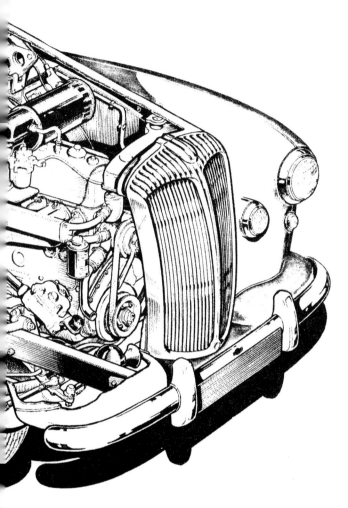

A VERY STURDY chassis frame, using massive cross-members, carries a modern pressed-steel body of attractive form. Suspension is by wishbones and torsion bars at the front and long semi-elliptics at the rear.

Two silencers are used in series and the whole exhaust system is carried on rubber-insulated brackets.

The cooling system employs a belt-driven two-blade fan and an impellor and the whole system is slightly pressurized by means of a spring-loaded overflow valve in the filler cap. Water jackets separate the bores, and the delivery from the pump is to the upper portion of the block, whence the water is directed upwards to the exhaust valve seats.

The cylinder block casting extends to the centre-line of the crankshaft, and pressed-in Brivadium dry liners, renewable after extended service, are used; as an interim measure, reboring up to a maximum 0.040 in. oversize is permissible.

Of the four-bearing type, the crankshaft is balanced statically and dynamically, and the increased rigidity resulting from a shorter stroke has made it possible to use only four balance weights instead of the previous six. The net result is a saving in weight of 26 lb. (the Conquest shaft turning the scale at 49½ lb.) as well as increased rigidity.

Cumulative Effect

At this point, it is worth mentioning that, throughout the design of this new engine, great attention has been paid to weight considerations, not by extensive use of light alloys, but by the elimination of surplus metal whenever that has proved possible without sacrifice of adequate safety margins, such components as the water impellor, fan pulleys and so on all having been designed with this end in view. In the aggregate, these efforts have provided a saving of approximately 1 cwt. over the weight of the Consort engine.

To revert to the crankshaft, the main bearings are of 2¼ in. diameter and the big ends 2 in., steel-backed white-metal liners being used in each case. On the nose of the crankshaft, a Metalastik torsional vibration damper is employed. The big ends are split diagonally to permit removal of the con. rods via the cylinder bores and the little ends incorporate a pinch-bolt location for the gudgeon pins. Very narrow rings (three compression and one scraper) are provided in the aluminium-alloy pistons.

Other engine details include a conventional force-feed lubrication system incorporating a Tecalemit full-flow filter and a gear-type pump driven by screw gearing from the camshaft, the same drive being extended upwards for the distributor, which has an over-riding hand vernier adjustment as well as centrifugal and vacuum control. The whole

the upper part, passing along the pipe and back along the lower passage.

Three advantages are claimed for this system; one is the obvious point that the engine quickly gets into its stride, since heat from the by-pass circuit is passed directly to the manifold; less obvious is the fact that even so-called cold water can give up a considerable amount of heat to provide the latent heat of vapourization required by carburation so that the initial chilling of the manifold is avoided; in addition, the water jacket also serves to limit the maximum mixture temperature by screening the manifold from the adjacent exhaust. A deflector plate is also used to screen the 42VIS downdraught Zenith carburetter, which incorporates an accelerating pump and a weakening device for cruising.

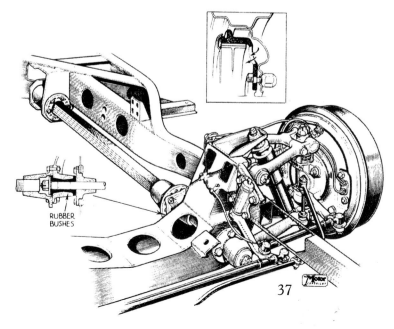

LAMINATED torsion bars are used for the front suspension in conjunction with wishbones of unequal length. Points which will be noted from this drawing are the vernier mountings of the torsion bars, the rubber bushes employed for the inner ends of the wishbones, the ventilated brake drums (inset), and the way in which the automatic chassis lubrication system is linked to the suspension and steering points which require lubricant.

RUBBER BUSHES

The Conquest—A New 2½-litre Daimler - - - Contd.

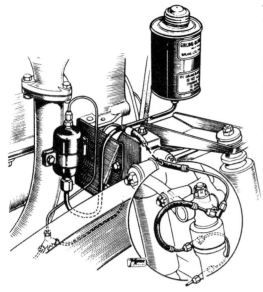

LABOUR SAVING.
—The Girling Bijur automatic chassis lubrication system incorporates a thermal pump mounted close to the exhaust. It draws lubricant from the reservoir on cooling and delivers it to 21 points on warming up. The inset shows the connections and metering orifices on the front suspension links and steering heads.

At the rear, long semi-elliptic springs are used and, at both ends of the chassis, the dampers are of the Girling telescopic type. Cushion tyres of large section (6.70 by 15) are fitted on 4½ J rims.

The Girling 2LS hydro-mechanical brakes operate in 11 in. drums with 1¾ in. wide linings, giving a generous friction area of 148 sq. in. In the interests of preventing squeak, the drums are machined all over and the webs of the shoes are slotted, whilst another unusual point is that each drum has eight 1⅛ in. diameter holes drilled near the periphery at points which are clear of the dished wheel hub flange; this (a normal Daimler feature) provides a distinct measure of ventilation and has been found to give a reduction in maximum drum temperature of nearly 50% on some models.

Pressed-steel construction is used for the attractively-styled body and the shell has an integral floor arranged to carry both the battery (which is under the rear seat) and the large fuel tank. Accommodation is of the four/five-seater order and, for actual dimensions, readers are referred to the diagrams which appear with the Road Test Report on page 444.

Interior furnishing conforms to traditional Daimler standards of quality, with walnut veneer for the generously-equipped facia board and the door cappings. High grade leather is used for the upholstery, which is simply carried out, with attractively piped cushions, but no superfluous ornamentation to detract from the air of quiet dignity.

The front seats are of the separately-adjustable close-up type, permitting three to be accommodated in an emergency, the central gearbox cover not obtruding excessively into the floor line. At the rear, the floor is so imperceptibly domed as to be virtually flat.

Comfort Features

All four doors are provided with arm rests, those at the front being adjustable, whilst there is also the usual folding centre arm rest at the back. In order to provide additional foot-room in the rear, the bases of the front squabs are cut away. Both front and rear doors are hinged on their leading edges and the handles are of the press-button type, whilst, conforming to usual Daimler practice, it is the near-side door which is locked by the ignition key.

As will be seen from the illustration, the car is notable for its large screen and window area. The windows have thin chromium-plated frames and hinged ventilating panels are fitted at the front, whilst the rear quarter lights are also hinged to provide an extractor effect for ventilation. So far as the latter is concerned, the Clayton heater and demister, built into the dash, is of the fresh-air type, drawing its supply from a scuttle ventilator which is unusual in having its aperture facing rearwards instead of forwards. A useful refinement is in the provision, on the facia, of a remote control for the water supply to the heater, as well as the usual rheostat switch for the fan.

Detail items of equipment include flush-fitting visors, small pockets in all doors, separate ash trays for all four occupants, a lockable glove box on the passenger's side of the instrument panel and a small cubby on the driver's side, a neat reducing type rear-view mirror, double-dipping headlamps supplemented by a pair of small built-in fog lamps, and provision on the facia board for a radio control panel.

Luggage accommodation takes the form of a large boot with top-hinged lid, the luggage platform providing a flat unobstructed surface, with the spare wheel and tools neatly housed below.

unit is three-point mounted on bonded rubber, the two front mountings being asymmetrical to allow for the fact that the c. of g. of the engine is not on the centre line.

So far as performance characteristics are concerned, the increase in maximum power output over the (slightly larger) 2½-litre Consort unit has already been stated, but equally important is the emphasis that has been placed on low-speed pulling powers, the engine showing the excellent b.m.e.p. figure of 124 at the low speed of 1,600 r.p.m. This characteristic is aimed at the dual objectives of brisk get-away on the fluid flywheel and notable acceleration on a 4.56:1 top-gear.

As already stated, the transmission incorporates the well-known Daimler fluid flywheel and epicyclic gearbox, with pre-selector control on the steering column, the remainder of the transmission line consisting of a Hardy Spicer open propeller shaft and Salisbury hypoid bevel axle.

The three grease nipples on the propeller shaft and one on the fan are the only grease nipples on the entire car, all other points (21 of them) which would normally require grease-gun attention being coupled to a Girling Bijur automatic system. This consists of an oil reservoir under the bonnet, which feeds a thermal pump mounted close to the exhaust pipe where it is affected by temperature changes of the latter; when this pump cools down, contraction draws in a fresh supply of oil, which is delivered (under an expansion pressure of about 4 lb. per sq. in.) via metered orifices to the various bearings when the pump warms up again. In practice, this means that all the points concerned are given their quota of oil every time the engine is started from cold.

Strongly Based

A conventional, but very sturdy chassis frame is used, with box-section longitudinals (2¼ in. wide and 5½ in. deep in the centre), linked by channel-section cruciform bracing and massive cross-members front and rear.

The front cross-member, which passes below the forward portion of the crankcase, also serves to carry the front suspension which follows the practice, initiated on the Lanchester Fourteen, of using laminated torsion bars and forged wishbones of unequal length. The points in favour of laminated torsion bars have been mentioned on previous occasions in *The Motor* and may be briefly enumerated as virtual freedom from risk of complete fracture, easier accommodation (owing to reduced length), lower cost and some degree of self-damping.

TWENTY reasons for the success
of the dashing Daimler CONQUEST

Over 80 m.p.h. plus Daimler dignity, for £1066 plus £445.5.10. p.t.

The engine is a 6 cylinder O.H.V. developing 75 b.h.p.

Top speed over 80, cruising 70.

Acceleration through the gears 0-30 in 5 seconds, 0-60 in 20.4 seconds, 10-30 in top 9.7 seconds. (Vide 'Motor' and 'Autocar' road test reports.)

Petrol 26.5 m.p.g. at 30 m.p.h., 18.5 m.p.g. at 70 m.p.h.

Fluid transmission (licensed under Vulcan-Sinclair and Daimler patents).

Preselector gear change with finger-tip control.

Automatic chassis lubrication.

*Independent front suspension provided by **laminated** torsion bars.*

A full-flow oil filter in the engine lubrication system.

11" brakes with 148 sq. in. surface.

33 ft. turning circle.

Armchair comfort in deeply cushioned seating with adjustable armrests.

Unobstructed flat floor.

Capacious luggage boot 4' × 3'.

Built-in heating and ventilating system included at *no* extra cost.

Front-hinged wide doors.

Extremely wide vision front and rear.

Superb appearance with high quality fittings.

Wide range of beautiful colour combinations.

Price £1066 plus £445.5.10 purchase tax.

SEE THE 'CONQUEST' AT THE MOTOR SHOW—STAND 164

If you are unable to visit the Show write for the free illustrated broadsheet and address of your nearest distributor to Bureau 2. The Daimler Company Limited, Coventry.

BY APPOINTMENT
Motor Car Manufacturers
to the late King George VI

'Out of pedigree comes pace'

THE DAIMLER COMPANY LIMITED COVENTRY

No. 1496 : DAIMLER CONQUEST SALOON

Although it is somewhat traditional in appearance, the new Daimler Conquest has well-balanced lines and a smart exterior style. The front wing line is swept back almost to the rear door ; and both front and rear wheels are exposed.

The Autocar ROAD TESTS

IN previous pages the newly introduced Daimler Conquest is described in detail; the model has also been made available for Road Test, so it is possible to record on the one occasion not only the menu but also the results that can be expected from the finished product. People who, in the past, have considered the products of the Daimler company as expensive or sedate luxury transport will need to revise their ideas, at least in part, in relation to this newcomer, as the Conquest, at £1,066 basic price, is not only good value for money, but also provides a very useful performance. Yet it retains a measure of Daimler refinement and detail finish that will satisfy the needs of the owner-driver who requires a car that is much above the average.

Briefly, the Conquest incorporates a new, relatively short-stroke 2½-litre six-cylinder engine which, together with a Daimler fluid flywheel and four-speed pre-selector gear box, is fitted in a slightly modified Lanchester chassis. A number of the body pressings are also similar to those used for the Lanchester, but the frontal treatment is a modern conversion of the traditional Daimler style, which retains the well-known fluted radiator grille. The result is a car that provides very comfortable transport for four persons. With a mean maximum speed of just over 80 m.p.h., together with an overall fuel consumption of almost 20 m.p.g. when driven fast, it can be cruised comfortably at around the 70 mark on the very accurate speedometer found on the car tested, without the engine showing the least sign of being overworked.

More important than sheer maximum speed is the way the car behaves under normal conditions and also how it accelerates. A high top speed is of little use on normal roads if a car requires several miles of straight road in order to reach the maximum. In this respect the Conquest is very satisfactory. Whilst also it is very flexible and has lively acceleration, well maintained through the speed range. It is difficult to say just how flexible the engine is, as the action of the fluid flywheel produces smooth-ness even with the most ham-fisted (and footed!) of drivers at the controls. On top gear the car will accelerate comfortably from speeds as low as 6 m.p.h., while it can even be smoothly started from rest on top gear. On the other hand, if the gears are freely used, acceleration from a stand-still to 60 m.p.h. can be accomplished in 20 seconds.

With a pre-selector gear box the method of driving, or more particularly of gear changing, differs from that used with a conventional arrangement. The gears are selected by a lever mounted on the steering column, but the actual engagement is performed by the pedal which is placed in the position usually occupied by the clutch pedal. Any desired gear can be selected by hand or pre-selected—in anticipation of requirements—but the change will not take place until the pedal is operated, and, following these operations, the car will not move (if it is already stationary) until the hand brake is released and the throttle is opened. Second gear is entirely satisfactory for normal starting from rest and its use for this purpose overcomes a slight tendency to creeping with first gear in use when waiting in traffic, though this is overcome by use of the hand brake or a touch on the brake pedal. This transmission arrangement, traditional to Daimler cars, results in a drive that provides a good measure of two-pedal control in dense traffic conditions. Generally, the change from gear to gear is very smooth, but some slight jerk can be provoked during a really fast change, such as is attempted, admittedly, by few drivers of a family type car.

Although a fairly conventional wishbone independent front suspension system is employed, a somewhat unusual arrangement of laminated torsion bars supports the car at

As well as a folding central armrest at the rear, combined door pulls and armrests are fitted to all doors. Ashtrays are placed in the backs of the front seats, and there are pull-out ashtrays in the front doors, in which are also small pockets. There is a lockable cupboard in the left of the facia, as well as a small open compartment to the right of the steering column.

The Conquest has a roomy luggage locker, but this does not result in an unduly bulbous appearance from the rear. Swivelling quarter lights are fitted at the front, while the windows behind the rear doors can also be opened slightly to increase ventilation. The fuel filler cap is placed horizontally on the left rear wing.

ROAD TEST . . . . continued

the front. This results in a fairly firm and well-controlled ride, and over all types of road surface the car handles well, although noise from regularly placed bumps in the road (such as cats' eyes) is quite noticeable, and tyre squeal can be produced at comparatively low cornering speeds. The roadholding is very good and the car has a feeling of general stability that inspires confidence. This is augmented by a slight understeer characteristic that is present even when the car is fully laden. There is very little roll on corners, and passengers remain almost unaffected by brisk cornering methods. This Daimler hugs the road in a manner that enables particularly good averages to be made even over twisty road sections. The steering is not specially low geared, and does not feel dead; it gives the driver a good idea of what the front wheels are doing, without being excessively heavy or transmitting shocks to his hands. The turning circle is good.

Hydro-mechanical brakes are used, and it is pleasing to record that not only do they perform well in normal driving conditions, but also that no fade was experienced under the very severe conditions imposed during the performance testing. A relatively heavy pedal pressure is required to exert the maximum stopping power, yet the required pedal pressure for normal check braking is not unduly heavy.

The general noise level of this car's progress is relatively low, and even at high speeds wind noise is not excessive. With the windows closed there are no hissing or whistling sounds that are sometimes produced by the edges of doors or quarterlights. The body is also well insulated and does not boom. Mechanically and as regards the exhaust, the engine is quiet; there is some sound from the transmission in the indirect ratios, of the type usually associated with this form of gear box and transmission, but this is not excessive.

The driving position is very good; both the cushion and the back rest of the separate seat are of adequate proportions and are well sprung. The seat gives plenty of support for the driver's back and legs, and even after very many hours of driving there are no aches that result from unsupported muscles. The position of the steering wheel and pedals relative to the seat is also well arranged. It would be better if there were a little more space between the clutch pedal and the hump in the floor over the transmission cover, to allow the dip switch to be placed in line with the other pedals. An organ-type throttle pedal is set at a comfortable angle and is smooth to operate. The gear-changing pedal requires about the same operating pressure as a normal clutch pedal, although the length of travel varies according to the gear that is selected.

Placed to the right of the steering column, the hand brake lever is well positioned and effective. Fore and aft adjustment of the front seats is controlled by a lever that is easy to operate; they can be set level to form virtually a single bench seat. From the driving seat it is just possible to see the opposite side front wing. The deep, curved one-piece windscreen provides unobstructed forward vision, and although the screen pillars are relatively thick they do not obstruct unduly. The rear view mirror is fairly small but it is very well placed and more than covers the area shown by the rear window.

Instruments and Minor Controls

All the instruments, minor controls and switches are grouped in the central section of the polished facia panel, the speedometer occupying the central position. Although this layout results in an attractive appearance, it would be better from a driving viewpoint if the instruments were grouped in front of the steering wheel. The position of the instruments prevents reflection from them in the windscreen, but the plated direction indicator switch does cause a slight reflection. An extra position on the lighting switch operates the fog lights and at the same time switches off the head lights. A valuable and now all too rare fuel reserve and a hand throttle control are fitted on the facia. There is a rheostat to control the brilliance of the instrument lighting, and a warning light is used to indicate low oil pressure—a device

This view shows the general layout of the engine and its auxiliaries. The heater unit—standard equipment on this model—is fitted to the bulkhead behind the engine. The radiator and oil filler caps, as well as the dipstick, are readily accessible. The tank to the left of the carburettor and above the steering column holds oil for the automatic chassis lubrication system.

The floor of the locker is covered with rubber to protect the luggage. A separate lower compartment houses the spare wheel and tools. The locker lid is spring loaded so that it remains in the open position when required.

that is more likely to attract the driver's attention from this all-important viewpoint than the normal gauge. Twin wipers cover a wide area of the windscreen and wipe it effectively; the blades are parked by switching off the electric motor when they are at the end of the stroke.

The high degree of comfort built into the front seats is also found in the rear compartment, where the seats are again of ample proportions; the rear seat back rests are extended unusually high and provide specially good support, while a central armrest gives transverse location to the passengers if the driver is in a hurry. With this armrest folded back it is possible to carry three persons in the rear compartment on occasions. Fitted as standard equipment, the heater system functions quite well and the circulation of air can be increased by opening the hinged rear quarter lights. There is a useful parcel tray behind the rear seat. Capacious pull-out ash trays are built into the front doors.

Double-dip head lamps give a satisfactory beam and a useful spread of light. The horns, operated by a central button on the steering wheel, are also up to the car's requirements. Starting from cold was good; the engine warmed up quickly and required little use of the mixture control. On initial starting in the garage, with a gear selected and engaged there is a slight tendency for the car to creep, even with the throttle closed, because of the higher engine idling speed applying with the mixture control in use. Automatic chassis lubrication reduces maintenance time to a minimum, as well as ensuring that the car receives a regular supply of lubricant, and there are only eight points that require individual lubrication (three of them every 1,000 miles).

The new Daimler Conquest is of particular interest to the owner-driver who requires a car with a very useful turn of acceleration and speed, together with a high degree of passenger comfort and detail finish.

DAIMLER CONQUEST SALOON

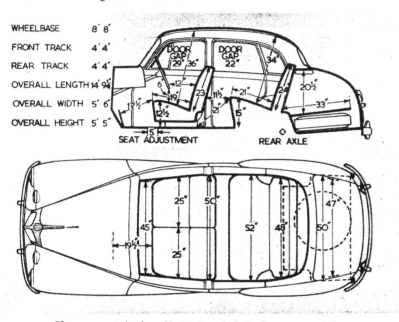

WHEELBASE	8' 8"
FRONT TRACK	4' 4"
REAR TRACK	4' 4"
OVERALL LENGTH	14' 9½"
OVERALL WIDTH	5' 6"
OVERALL HEIGHT	5' 5"

Measurements in these ¼in to 1ft scale body diagrams are taken with the driving seat in the central position of fore and aft adjustment and with the seat cushions uncompressed.

─── DATA ───

PRICE (basic), with saloon body, £1,066.
British purchase tax, £445 5s 10d.
Total (in Great Britain), £1,511 5s 10d.
Extras: Radio, £38 1s 6d.

ENGINE: Capacity: 2,433 c.c. (148.4 cu in).
Number of cylinders: 6.
Bore and stroke: 76.2 × 88.9 mm (3 × 3½in).
Valve gear: Overhead, push rods.
Compression ratio: 6.6 to 1.
B.H.P.: 75 at 4,000 r.p.m. (B.H.P. per ton laden, 47.6).
Torque: 124 lb ft at 2,000 r.p.m.
M.P.H. per 1,000 r.p.m. on top gear, 17.4.

WEIGHT (with 5 gals. fuel), 27¾ cwt (3,100 lb).
Weight distribution (per cent) 50.3 F; 49.7 R.
Laden as tested: 31¼ cwt (3,514 lb).
Lb per c.c. (laden): 1.44.

BRAKES: Type: F, Two-leading shoe. R, leading and trailing.
Method of operation: F, Hydraulic. R, Mechanical.
Drum dimensions: F, 11in diameter, 1¾in wide. R, 11in diameter, 1¾in wide.
Lining area: F, 70.3 sq in. R, 70.5 sq in. (89.5 sq in per ton laden).

TYRES: 6.70-15in.
Pressures (lb per sq in): 24 F; 24 R.

TANK CAPACITY: 15 Imperial gallons (including 1½ gallons reserve).
Oil sump, 10 pints.
Cooling system, 18 pints.

TURNING CIRCLE: 34ft 0in (L and R).
Steering wheel turns (lock to lock): 3¼.
DIMENSIONS: Wheelbase 8ft 8in.
Track: 4ft 4in (F); 4ft 4in (R).
Length (overall): 14ft 9½in.
Height: 5ft 5in.
Width: 5ft 6in.
Ground clearance: 7in.
Frontal area: 22.3 sq ft (approximately).

ELECTRICAL SYSTEM: 12 volt; 51 ampère-hour battery.
Head lights: Double dip, 42-36 watt.

SUSPENSION: Front, Independent; wishbones and torsion bars. Anti-roll bar. Rear, Half-elliptic springs.

─── PERFORMANCE ───

ACCELERATION: from constant speeds.
Speed, Gear Ratios and time in sec.

M.P.H.	4.56 to 1	6.71 to 1	10.05 to 1	17.47 to 1
10—30	9.7	6.9	5.3	—
20—40	10.1	7.2	—	—
30—50	10.8	8.3	—	—
40—60	12.8	—	—	—
50—70	15.5	—	—	—

From rest through gears to:

M.P.H.			sec
30	..	..	4.9
50	..	..	13.0
60	..	..	20.4
70	..	..	30.0

Standing quarter mile, 22.3 sec.

SPEED ON GEARS:

Gear			M.P.H. (normal and max.)	K.P.H. (normal and max.)
Top	..	(mean)	80.5	129.6
		(best)	81.0	130.4
3rd	..	..	50—60	80—97
2nd	..	..	30—39	48—63
1st	..	..	16—22	26—35

TRACTIVE RESISTANCE: 39 lb per ton at 10 M.P.H.

SPEEDOMETER CORRECTION: M.P.H.

Car speedometer:	..	..	..	10	20	30	40	50	60	70	80	82.5
True speed:	..	..	..	10.5	20	30	39	48	59	68.5	78.5	81

TRACTIVE EFFORT:

			Pull (lb per ton)	Equivalent Gradient
Top	..	..	233	1 in 9.6
Third	..	..	323	1 in 6.8
Second	..	..	405	1 in 5.4

BRAKES:

Efficiency	Pedal Pressure (lb)
82 per cent	140
70 per cent	100
45 per cent	60

FUEL CONSUMPTION:
19.7 m.p.g. overall for 544 miles (14.3 litres per 100 km).
Approximate normal range 19–22 m.p.g. (14.9–12.8 litres per 100 km).
Fuel, First grade.

WEATHER: Dry; wind slight.
Air temperature 62 degrees F.
Acceleration figures are the means of several runs in opposite directions.
Tractive effort and resistance obtained by Tapley meter.
Model described in The Autocar of May 8, 1953.

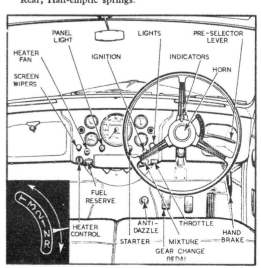

NOW
is the time to order your Daimler
CONQUEST

OVER 80 M.P.H. PLUS DAIMLER DIGNITY FOR £1,066 PLUS £445.5.10 P/T.

THE DAIMLER 'CONQUEST' was an instant success on its introduction and, although Factory production has been constantly stepped up to shorten the delivery period, it will still be some time before we can offer immediate delivery, although the position is rapidly improving.

You will be well advised to place your order for your 'Conquest' now, *especially as there will be no alteration in specification or price of the 'Conquest' to be featured at this year's Motor Show.* Order now, therefore, and avoid the post-show waiting list!

To obtain the complete inside information on this remarkable car and the name and address of your nearest distributor you should write today for the free fully illustrated broadsheet to **BUREAU 2, THE DAIMLER CO. LTD., COVENTRY.**

BY APPOINTMENT
The Daimler Co. Limited
Motor Car Manufacturers
to the late King George VI

'OUT OF PEDIGREE COMES PACE'

Why so many motorists and their wives are choosing the Daimler CONQUEST

OVER 80 M.P.H. PLUS DAIMLER DIGNITY FOR £1066 PLUS £445.5.10 P/T.

Since its dramatic debut in May of this year, the Daimler 'CONQUEST' has enjoyed the most spectacular success, and for the very best of reasons. It fulfils the demands of the greatest number of different kinds of motorists, from the critical enthusiast to the cautious beginner.

The fast driver. For the driver who likes to feel urge and power under his right foot, who prefers to be off first at the lights, the 'CONQUEST' leaps from 0-30 in 5 secs., 0-60 in 20.4 secs. through the gears, and from 10-30 in 9.7 secs. in top. (Vide 'Motor' and 'Autocar' road test reports). Top speed is over 80, cruising 70.

The take-it-easy driver. One of the features sure to appeal to the driver who likes to take things easy is the fluid transmission, cunningly in league with a preselector gearchange. This allows great top-gear flexibility and easy traffic crawling, and virtually two-pedal control at all times.

The 'family' driver. The roomy interior with its wide, deep seating, its ample leg room and unobstructed flat floor gives really comfortable accommodation for a family of five or six. The large luggage boot measures 3′ × 4′. Independent front suspension is provided by *laminated* torsion bars and completely cancels out roll and sway, even on fast cornering.

Points for the record. The 'CONQUEST's' 2½ litre engine is a 6 cylinder O.H.V. developing 75 b.h.p. ● Petrol consumption from 26.5 m.p.g. at 30 m.p.h. to 18.5 m.p.g. at 70 m.p.h. ● Automatic chassis lubrication. ● 11″ brakes with area of 148 sq. ins.

The price of the 'CONQUEST' is £1066 plus £445.5.10 p/t. This is less than most knowledgeable motorists will expect from such a combination of pace, performance and pedigree with the name of Daimler.

*　　*　　*　　*　　*

To obtain full details of the remarkable Daimler 'CONQUEST' and the address of your nearest distributor you should write today for the free illustrated broadsheet to Bureau 2, The Daimler Company Limited, Coventry.

'OUT OF PEDIGREE COMES PACE'

The 2½-litre Daimler Conquest

ELSEWHERE in this issue we describe in detail the new 2½-litre Daimler Conquest saloon, which makes its bow to the public today and takes the place of the former 2½-litre Consort model. Here we are able to give a detailed Road Test Report based on some 800 miles of pre-announcement motoring in the new model, during the course of which full-scale performance tests were carried out.

Two points very soon emerged. One is that, despite this car being· expressly designed for the more-stringent economy of the post-war world, it is still unmistakably in the Daimler tradition; the other is that it is in every way a better performer than the previous 2½-litre Consort and, by any standards, a notably lively example of its class.

Performance being a matter on which considerable importance is placed by many present-day motorists, the latter aspects may well be dealt with first by a few key comparisons. The new car is over 5% faster than the old, with a mean figure of 81.6 m.p.h., which is not only creditable by comparison with the Consort, but is notably high for any roomy and comfortable car in the 2-2½-litre class and is particularly praiseworthy in view of the outstanding top-gear flexibility—a point on which much more will be said later.

Good Acceleration

Here, it may be recorded that the top-gear acceleration figures for the Conquest represent improvements ranging from 11.4% to no less than 31% compared with the Consort, the car being one of the comparatively few medium-powered models of essentially touring type which is capable of accelerating from 10 m.p.h. to 30 m.p.h. in under ten seconds. The top-gear characteristics of this model do not shine merely at low speeds, moreover, the liveliness being maintained throughout the range, as an examination of the detailed figures will show.

In the matter of standing-start acceleration times through the gears, the Conquest also shows up well although, in this case,

New Medium-powered Model from Old-established Factory Proves an Outstanding Top-gear Performer with Very Lively Acceleration and High Maximum Speed

it is apposite to point out that cars with fluid flywheels tend to do themselves less than justice by the hard criterion of figures, since a fluid coupling inevitably imposes an initial limit on engine revs., thereby preventing the semi-racing start possible with a friction clutch. In practice, of course, this is of comparatively little importance, since few drivers ever start in the latter manner.

So far as fuel consumption is concerned, the constant-speed readings obtained with the Conquest proved identical with those of the Consort at some speeds and better at others, notably at the top end of the speed range where the Conquest showed an improvement of 2 m.p.g. at 70 m.p.h. The car tested, incidentally, was an early example with the standard compression ratio of 6.6 to 1, and better consumption figures (as well as improved general performance) are to be expected from the 6.75 to 1 ratio which is at present the subject of experiment and which may be adopted now that premium fuels are available.

So much for pure comparisons which, although showing up the new model to very distinct all-round advantage, in-

evitably tell only a part of the story. Mention was made earlier of the flexibility of this new engine and this point cannot be stressed too highly. Although no-one would wish to do so in view of the absurdly easy gear changes provided by the pre-selector transmission, it is quite possible to drive through a busy town without ever moving the gear lever out of the top-gear notch or depressing the gear-changing pedal. So well is the fluid flywheel mated to the torque characteristics of the engine that the car will move off from rest with top gear engaged without even an expert driver being able to detect the point at which fluid slip ceases and the engine takes over entirely. Although such treatment is putting the engine and transmission to the extreme test, the fact that the car behaves impeccably when treated in this way is clear proof that the degree to which a Conquest driver hangs on to top gear is more a reflection of the laziness of his mood than a measure of his mechanical brutality.

Low-speed Power

We, ourselves, found a strong temptation to amble through traffic in this leisurely fashion when no need for hurry existed, the more so as the low-speed pulling powers of the new short-stroke six-cylinder engine are so notably good, the car being capable of easily bettering a gradient of 1 in 10 on top gear.

As with previous models, however, this Daimler is a car which adapts itself quite remarkably to its driver's moods. When in a hurry, one can treat it in distinctly sporting fashion, using the gears to the full and taking advantage of the rapid and easy change offered by the pre-selector transmission. The latter, of course, is delightful in the way it enables a driver to anticipate his future needs

QUALITY appointments include walnut veneered facia panel and door cappings, high-grade leather upholstery and conveniently placed ashtrays and arm-rests. Front-hinged doors, ample window areas and individual front seats are other notable points.

The 2½-litre Daimler Conquest   -   -   Contd.

A CURVED rear window of ample width surmounts the capacious luggage locker beneath the forward-sloping floor of which is separate accommodation for the spare wheel and tools.

and act on them only at the psychological moment.

Thus one can place the steering column lever (which can be operated by the finger tips without moving the hand from the wheel) in the third-gear position in anticipation of overtaking a car in front and leave the actual change, effected by merely depressing and releasing the gear-changing pedal, until the exact moment when the road ahead becomes clear. In practice, changing down is seldom necessary for overtaking, thanks to the extremely good top-gear acceleration, but a comfortable third-gear speed of 50 m.p.h. is at the driver's disposal if required.

So far as top-gear cruising is concerned, the Conquest will maintain a very willing 70 m.p.h., with a useful amount of throttle in hand. At this pace, one is conscious that the engine is turning over at a comparatively high speed (4,000 r.p.m.) and although there is no noticeable vibration, some drivers would, perhaps, prefer rather higher gearing, although this would naturally somewhat reduce the outstanding top-gear flexibility.

Other characteristics of the engine are easy starting and quick warming-up, whilst an unusual refinement is the provision of a hand throttle which enables the engine to be set at a fast idle without use of the actual choke. Further good points are ready accessibility *via* the counterbalanced bonnet, and the provision of a very long dipstick which enables the oil level to be checked without risk of soiling clothes.

The braking figures (which show high efficiencies at low pedal pressures) may be allowed to speak for themselves, the only point for comment being a slight tendency to low-speed squeak from one front drum, the fact that only one drum offended suggesting that the fault was probably particular to the model concerned rather than to the type.

On the car tried, overseas damper settings were used and these gave quite unusually firm suspension by present-day i.f.s. standards, a characteristic which many will like, although others would undoubtedly prefer the greater bump absorption at low speeds which can be expected from softer settings. Either way, the suspension is free from vices and the general handling of the car is notably good.

There is normally a mild degree of understeer, and corners can be taken at fast touring speeds with the utmost confidence. The same applies to really fast cornering although, in this case, the Conquest is slightly more sensitive than some to changing camber.

The steering lock is exceptionally good for a car of its size and the gearing employed gives light control under normal cruising conditions, although calling for moderate effort at low speeds. Elimination of road shocks on the wheel has been effected to a reasonable degree.

Interior Planning

Very good marks must be awarded for the layout of the controls (apart from a rather awkwardly-placed foot dipper) and also for the instruments (speedometer, petrol gauge, clock, ammeter and thermometer) which have very clear circular dials and are cleverly illuminated from behind at night so that the figures show white and the faces a dark grey, against which the hands can be distinguished in silhouette, the effect being clear and glareless, with the additional refinement of a rheostat control for suiting individual tastes. Warning lights are used for the ignition and oil pressure and an appreciated minor luxury is a petrol reserve control. This gives a 1½-gallon emergency supply and the total tankage provides a range of rather more than 300 miles.

High praise can also be given for visibility, which is notably good for all the occupants, points playing an important part in this respect being the deep screen (which enables the occupants of the rear compartment to have a good view ahead, as well as those in front) and the rear quarter lights (which give a wide lateral range of vision from the rear seats as well as helping the driver when manœuvring). The rear-view mirror, of the reducing type, gives a clear picture astern and causes a minimum of obstruction to forward vision.

Provision for ventilation is comprehensive, with hinged panels on the front doors and hinged quarter lights. Despite this, however, the Conquest is not above criticism on the score of wind noise at high cruising speeds if a reasonable degree of ventilation is required: hinged panels on the front doors invariably make some roar or whistle at high speed and the alternative of lowering the window offers no relief in this case, since the window is tapered and arranged so that the glass comes clear of the rear of the frame, instead of the front, which is an arrangement seemingly more conducive to the production of wind noise. A reasonable compromise for cold weather is to rely on the heater air intake for fresh air and the quarter lights for extraction, but this is hardly adequate for warm days.

In appearance, the Conquest follows typical Daimler lines and the air of solid comfort which characterizes the whole car is not belied by the satisfaction it gives to driver and passengers. The finish is excellent, without in any way being ostentatious. The same attention to detail applies to individual fittings and furnishings, all of which are carried out efficiently and in good quality. From an owner-driver angle, the automatic chassis lubrication system is a feature which is, unfortunately, all too rare today, and another detail of note is the provision of twin built-in fog lamps controlled from the normal light switch—the latter, incidentally, well up to the car's performance.

The Daimler company has always paid special attention to seating comfort and the Conquest is a most worthy example of the line, the seats, at both front and back, offering really excellent all-round support in a posture entirely appropriate to both driving and "passengering." Indeed, this is a car in which one can sit in either front or rear seats for quite exceptionally long periods without fatigue.

The quality and finish of the appointments add mental satisfaction to the physical comfort offered by the interior and, coupled with the general liveliness and quite outstanding top-gear performance, make the Conquest a model which will find many friends.

The Motor Road Test No. 6/53

Make : Daimler   **Type :** Conquest
Makers : The Daimler Co. Ltd., Coventry

Dimensions and Seating

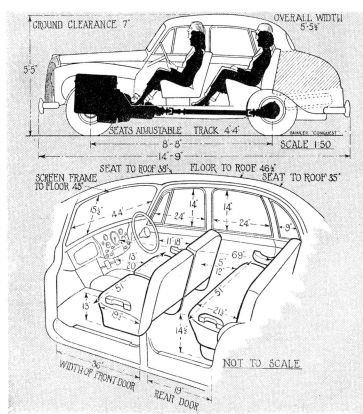

GROUND CLEARANCE 7" · OVERALL WIDTH 5'5½" · 5'5" · SEATS ADJUSTABLE · TRACK 4'4" · DAIMLER "CONQUEST" · 8'8" · 14'-9" · SCALE 1:50

SCREEN FRAME TO FLOOR 43" · SEAT TO ROOF 38½" · FLOOR TO ROOF 46½" · SEAT TO ROOF 35" · 15½" · 4'4" · 14" · 24" · 14" · 24" · 9" · 11'18" · 13" · 20" · 69" · 5" · 12" · 5" · 13" · 19½" · 21½" · 14½" · WIDTH OF FRONT DOOR 36" · REAR DOOR 19" · NOT TO SCALE

In Brief

Price : £1,066 plus purchase tax £445 5s. 10d. equals £1,511 5s. 10d.
Capacity .. .. .. 2,433 c.c.
Unladen kerb weight .. 28 cwt.
Fuel consumption :
  (driven hard) .. .. 20.3 m.p.g.
Maximum speed .. .. 81.6 m.p.h.
Maximum speed on 1 in 20
  gradient .. .. 67 m.p.h.
Maximum top gear gradient 1 in 8.9.
Acceleration :
  10-30 m.p.h. in top .. 9.7 sec.
  0-50 m.p.h. through gears 16.3 sec.
Gearing : 17.4 m.p.h. in top at 1,000 r.p.m., 75 m.p.h. at 2,500 ft. per min. piston speed.

Specification

Engine
Cylinders 6
Bore .. .. 76.2 mm.
Stroke .. .. 88.9 mm.
Cubic capacity .. .. 2,433 c.c.
Piston area .. .. 42.4 sq. in.
Valves .. .. Overhead (push rod)
Compression ratio 6.6/1
Max. power .. .. .. 75 b.h.p.
  at .. .. .. 4,000 r.p.m.
Piston speed at max. b.h.p. 2,330 ft. per min.
Carburetter .. Zenith downdraught 42 VIS
Ignition .. .. .. Lucas coil
Sparking plugs .. 14 mm. Lodge CLN
Fuel pump .. .. AC mechanical
Oil filter .. .. Tecalemit full-flow
Transmission
Clutch .. (Daimler fluid flywheel)
  .. pre-selector gearbox)
Top gear 4.56
3rd gear 6.71
2nd gear 10.05
1st gear 17.47
Propeller shaft .. Hardy Spicer, open
Final drive .. .. Hypoid bevel
Chassis
Brakes .. .. Girling Hydro-mechanical
           (2LS on front)
Brake drum diameter .. .. 11 in.
Friction lining area .. .. 148 sq. in.
Suspension :
  Front : Independent (laminated torsion bars)
  Rear .. ..Semi-elliptic
Shock absorbers :
  Front .. .. Girling telescopic (DAS 4)
  Rear .. .. Girling telescopic (DAS 6/40)
Tyres .. .. Dunlop Cushion, 6.70 × 15
Steering
Steering gear .. .. Bishop Cam (18:1 ratio)
Turning circle .. .. .. 34 ft.
Turns of steering wheel, lock to lock .. 3¼
Performance factors (at laden weight as tested)
Piston area, sq. in. per ton .. 26.9
Brake lining area, sq. in. per ton .. 94.0
Specific displacement, litres per ton mile 2,690
(Fully described in this issue of " The Motor.")

Maintenance

Fuel tank : 15 gallons (incl. 1½ reserve). **Sump :** 10 pints, S.A.E. 30. **Gearbox :** 5½ pints, S.A.E. 30. **Rear Axle :** 2½ pints, S.A.E. 90 E.P. **Steering Gear :** 1½ pints, S.A.E. 90 E.P. **Radiator :** 18 pints (3 drain taps). **Chassis lubrication :** Automatic thermal system to 21 points : by oil gun to prop. shaft (3 points) every 1,000 miles and by grease gun to water pump (1 point) every 3,000 miles. **Ignition timing :** 9° B.T.D.C. **Spark Plug gap :** 0.020 in. **Contact breaker gap :** 0.014—0.016 in. **Valve timing :** Inlet opens 17° B.T.D.C. and closes 55° A.B.D.C. Exhaust opens 50° B.B.D.C. and closes 22° A.T.D.C. **Tappet clearances** (Hot) : Inlet 0.013 in. Exhaust 0.013 in. **Front wheel toe-in :** ⅛ in. **Camber angle :** 1½°. **Castor angle :** Zero. **Tyre pressures :** Front 24 lb., Rear 24 lb. (or 26 lb. for exceptional load) **Brake Fluid :** Girling Crimson. **Battery :** 12-volt 51 amp./hr. (Lucas G.T.W.9A). **Lamp bulbs :** Headlamps, 42/36 watt. Lucas No. 354. Sidelamps, 6 watt. Lucas No. 207. Stop and tail lamps, 18/6 watt. Lucas No. 361. No. plate lamp 6 watt, Lucas No. 989. Reversing light, 18 watt, Lucas No. 221. Fog lamps, 38 watt, Lucas No. 325. Roof lamp, 6 watt, Lucas No. 254.

Ref. B 25/53

Test Conditions

Weather : Cool, dry with light wind blowing across course.   Surface : Dry tar macadam. Fuel : Premium grade.

Test Data

ACCELERATION TIMES on Two Upper Ratios

	Top	3rd.
10-30 m.p.h.	9.7 sec.	6.5 sec.
20-40 m.p.h.	10.0 sec.	7.3 sec.
30-40 m.p.h.	11.6 sec.	9.4 sec.
40-60 m.p.h.	12.8 sec.	—
50-70 m.p.h.	18.5 sec.	—

ACCELERATION TIMES Through Gears

0-30 m.p.h.	7.0 sec.
0-40 m.p.h.	11.4 sec.
0-50 m.p.h.	16.3 sec.
0-60 m.p.h.	24.3 sec.
0-70 m.p.h.	36.2 sec.
Standing Quarter Mile	23.2 sec.

FUEL CONSUMPTION

26.5 m.p.g. at constant 30 m.p.h.
25.0 m.p.g. at constant 40 m.p.h.
23.0 m.p.g. at constant 50 m.p.h.
21.0 m.p.g. at constant 60 m.p.h.
18.5 m.p.g. at constant 70 m.p.h.
Overall consumption (driven hard) for 325 miles, 16 gallons=20.3 m.p.g.

HILL CLIMBING (At steady speeds)

Max. top gear speed on 1 in 20	.. .. ..	67 m.p.h.
Max. top gear speed on 1 in 15	.. .. ..	63 m.p.h.
Max. top gear speed on 1 in 10	.. .. ..	43 m.p.h.
Max. gradient on top gear	.. ..	1 in 8.9 (Tapley 250 lb./ton)
Max. gradient on 3rd. gear	.. ..	1 in 6.3 (Tapley 350 lb./ton)
Max. gradient on 2nd gear	.. ..	1 in 4.8 (Tapley 460 lb./ton)

BRAKES at 30 m.p.h.

0.98 g retardation (=31 ft. stopping distance) with 100 lb. pedal pressure
0.94 g retardation (=32 ft. stopping distance) with 75 lb. pedal pressure
0.70 g retardation (=43 ft. stopping distance) with 50 lb. pedal pressure
0.32 g retardation (=94 ft. stopping distance) with 25 lb. pedal pressure

MAXIMUM SPEEDS
Flying Quarter-mile

Mean of four opposite runs .. 81.6 m.p.h.
Best time equals .. .. .. 81.8 m.p.h.

Speed in gears

Max. speed in 3rd gear .. .. 61 m.p.h.
Max. speed in 2nd gear .. .. 38 m.p.h.
Max. speed in 1st gear .. .. 22 m.p.h.

WEIGHT

Unladen kerb weight .. .. 28 cwt.
Front/rear weight distribution .. 52/48
Weight laden as tested .. .. 31½ cwt.

INSTRUMENTS

Speedometer at 30 m.p.h. .. .. 1% fast
Speedometer at 60 m.p.h. .. .. 4% fast
Distance recorder .. .. .. 1% fast

OUT OF PEDIGREE COMES PACE!

The success of the Daimler CONQUEST

DAIMLER DIGNITY PLUS DASH IS

THE TALK OF THE TOWN

In the short time that the CONQUEST has been on the market at the medium price of £1511.5.10 including purchase tax, it has become a major talking point in motoring circles all over the country. It is unmistakably a Daimler for its dignity and graciousness. It is also a car of verve and dash, with a ready aptitude to leap from nought to thirty in 5 seconds —on to sixty in a further 15½ seconds —soon reaching and holding without effort a speed of well over eighty.

Daimler fluid transmission*

This thoroughbred performance is held in very nice control by fluid flywheel transmission and preselector gearbox—a unique Daimler combination that is a joy to handle at any time, but really comes into its own when weaving through difficult traffic.

NOTE THE DAIMLER FLAT FLOOR

THE PRIDE OF THE COUNTRY

Add to all this a roomy interior, the Daimler flat floor, and a suspension that gives passengers very little intimation of high speed, cornering or rough going, and it is easy to understand why the CONQUEST has been welcomed with such enthusiasm.

Test the 'CONQUEST'

May we suggest that you call on your nearest Daimler dealer for a personal trial of the CONQUEST. For your records, other salient details of the CONQUEST are: 6 cylinder O.H.V. engine—75 b.h.p. • Petrol consumption 23 m.p.g. (at constant 50 m.p.h.) Independent front wheel suspension provided by *laminated* torsion bars • Automatic chassis lubrication • Girling brakes on 11″ drums with area of 148 sq. ins.

Licensed under Vulcan-Sinclair and Daimler patents.

A fully descriptive broadsheet is available free on request to The Daimler Co. Ltd., Bureau 2, Coventry

BY APPOINTMENT
The Daimler Co. Limited
Motor Car Manufacturers
to the late King George VI

GIRLING EQUIPMENT ON THE

DAIMLER

DJ250 & 251 Conquest Saloon
DJ252 & 253 Conquest Century Coupe
DJ254 & 255 Conquest Century Roadster
DJ256 & 257 Conquest Century Saloon
DF304 & 305 Regency
1953-56

MODEL	
DJ250 & 251 Saloon	
FRONT BRAKES	REAR BRAKES
$11 \times 1\frac{3}{4}$ HLSS Section 2, Page 51	$11 \times 1\frac{3}{4}$ GNSS Section 2, Page 5

MODEL	
DJ252/3/4/5 & 6 Coupe, Roadster and Saloon	
FRONT BRAKES	REAR BRAKES
$11 \times 2\frac{1}{4}$ HLSS Section 2, Page 51	$11 \times 2\frac{1}{4}$ GNSS Section 2, Page 5
BRAKE MASTER CYLINDER (above models)	
$\frac{7}{8}$in. Tension Type Section 3, Page 9	

MODEL	
DF304 & 305 Regency	
FRONT BRAKE	REAR BRAKES
$12 \times 2\frac{1}{4}$ HLSS Section 2, Page 51	$12 \times 2\frac{1}{4}$ GNSS Section 2, Page 5
BRAKE MASTER CYLINDER	
1in. Tension Type Section 3, Page 9	
SUPPLY TANK (all models)	
Single Feed (Metal) Section 3, Page 19	

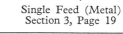

A GREAT DAIMLER DOUBLE

The dashing and successful Daimler
CONQUEST

The remarkable Daimler Conquest is already famous for bringing to the medium price market a brilliant combination of Daimler dignity and dash. A speed of over 80, fluid transmission, preselector gearchange, automatic chassis lubrication and *laminated* torsion bars have combined to create an entirely new concept of motoring. Price £1066 plus £445.5.10 purchase tax.

...and now the new
CONQUEST 'CENTURY'

Price of the
CONQUEST 'CENTURY'
£1172. 0. 0
plus
£489. 9. 2 *p.t.*

The Conquest 'Century' will appeal especially to those who appreciate the extraordinary combination of grace and speed in the Conquest, but who would like just that much extra power and a number of additional refinements. The special series engine develops 100 b.h.p. and has twin carburettors. Acceleration is even quicker and top speed is over 90 m.p.h. Brakes are ½″ wider to cope with the extra speed. Extras on the Conquest 'Century' include bigger bumpers; new instrument panel with revolution counter; telescopic adjustable steering; improved seating and more leg room in rear; foam rubber upholstery; two suitcases specially designed to fit boot; strap hangers; chromium plated frames for windscreen and rear windows. *For address of nearest distributor write to Bureau C2, The Daimler Co. Ltd. Coventry.*

D221

OUT OF PEDIGREE COMES PACE

1954 CARS

The Daimler Conquest

An Additional Model Offering Higher Performance, More Leg-room at the Rear, and Extra Equipment

Unusual in these days of large luggage boots and small rear compartments is the ample leg room provided for rear seat passengers on the Conquest Century, even when the driver's seat is well back on its adjustment.

The redesigned instrument panel with the speedometer on the right and the rev. counter on the left, and the enlarged steering wheel are features of the Century cockpit.

SINCE its introduction last May, the Daimler Conquest has proved itself admirably suited to the day-to-day requirements of business and professional men, both at home and abroad. Now, a more highly-developed version of the Conquest has been introduced to meet the needs of the keen motorist who wants a car with an even higher performance than the 80 m.p.h.-plus maximum of the standard saloon and who requires a car fully equipped for long distance touring. Known as the Conquest Century, the new model supplements but does not replace the standard Conquest saloon. Basic price of the Conquest Century is £1,172, and its total price including purchase tax is £1,661 9s. 2d.

Naturally, the new model greatly resembles the standard Conquest saloon on which it is based, but under the bonnet the Century owes much to the development work carried out on the Conquest engine for installation in the 100-m.p.h. Daimler Roadster, which was one of the surprises of the 1953 Motor Show.

Like the Roadster, the Conquest Century engine has an aluminium cylinder head instead of the cast iron pattern fitted to the Conquest. It also has the Roadster's 7.75 to 1 compression ratio instead of the standard 7 to 1 ratio, the inlet and exhaust valves larger by $\frac{1}{8}$ in., the twin S.U. horizontal carburetters and the high-lift camshaft. As a result of these modifications, the 2,433 c.c. six-cylinder engine develops 100 b.h.p. at 4,400 r.p.m. compared with the 75 b.h.p. produced by the standard engine at 4,000 r.p.m. As this latter output is sufficient to give the normal Conquest saloon a maximum speed of 81.6 m.p.h. and enables it to accelerate from 0 to 50 m.p.h. in 16.3 sec., the 33% increase should make the Century version of the Conquest a somewhat difficult car to overtake.

It is expected that many drivers will take full advantage

of the increased power output of the engine, and steps have therefore been taken to ensure that the transmission shall be equal to the new demands now being made on it. The propeller shaft has been increased in diameter from $2\frac{1}{2}$ in. to $2\frac{3}{4}$ in. and the normal two-star differential has been replaced by one of the four-star type.

Good brakes are essential if the higher performance is to be usable in safety, and the drums of the Girling Hydro-mechanical brakes have therefore been increased in width by half an inch, thereby increasing the friction lining area from 148 sq. in. to 184 sq. in.

No other departures from the standard specification of the chassis have been made, and the new model retains all the outstanding Conquest features including independent front suspension by laminated torsion bars and unequal length wishbones, the famous Daimler transmission system of a fluid flywheel operating in conjunction with an epicyclic gear box, with pre-selector control, and the Girling Bijur automatic lubrication system.

There is, therefore, little in the new model which has not already been tried and tested in the hands of thousands of owners. Even the new chassis features have already proved their worth in arduous conditions, for they were all incorporated in the seven Daimler Conquests which competed in the 1954 Monte-Carlo Rally. It will be recalled that no fewer than five of the seven cars finished in the first hundred, and the performance and handling of these five cars during the five-lap high-speed

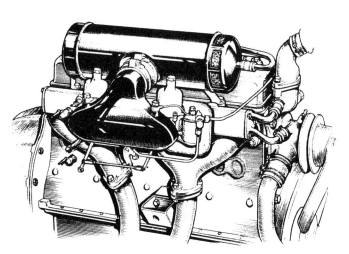

Gas flow is aided by the fitting of two S.U. horizontal carburetters on an unusual water-heated manifold now characteristic of Daimler design, and by the adoption of a two-branch exhaust manifold.

entury Saloon

Distinguishing features in this view of the Daimler Conquest Century are its deeper bumpers, the chromium surround for the windscreen and the narrow anti-draught strip at the rear of the front window.

test on the difficult Monaco Grand Prix circuit greatly impressed the many knowledgeable spectators present.

Only the most lynx-eyed car spotter will be able to distinguish between the Conquest and the Conquest Century from most angles, for few exterior alterations have been made to the body. At the front of the car the windscreen surround is now of chromed metal instead of black rubber. Vertical strips of glass at the rear of the front windows have been added to act as draught excluders, and the rear light also has a chromium surround. The rear of an overtaking Century is also identifiable by a chromium motif on the boot lid above which appear the words "Daimler" in chromium letters. Incidentally, this is believed to be the first Daimler model to carry the name of its manufacturers.

Making More Room

Most important interior modification to the body is the re-positioning of the rear seat further back in the body to give four inches more leg room for the rear passengers. The result is that, even when a long-legged driver is occupying the driving seat and has pushed it sufficiently far back to make himself comfortable, there is still ample leg room for a six-foot rear passenger.

At the front of the car the addition of a rev. counter to the speedometer, petrol gauge, clock, ammeter and thermometer normally fitted has been accomplished by a rearrangement of the instruments, the speedometer now being on the right of the panel and therefore nearer the driver's line of vision than when in its normal position in the centre. The rev. counter has been placed on the extreme left of the panel where it is rather out of the line of sight of the driver. A very welcome addition to the Century model of the Conquest is a telescopic steering column, while the provision of an 18-in. steering wheel instead of the 17-in. wheel normally fitted gives just that extra sense of control so valuable for the handling of a high-performance car. This feeling of being very much in control of things is aided also by the squabs of the front seats which, on the Century, are shaped to

DAIMLER "CONQUEST CENTURY" DATA

Engine dimensions			Chassis details	
Cylinders		6	Brakes	Girling Hydro-mechanical (2LS on front)
Bore		76.2 mm.		
Stroke		88.9 mm.		
Cubic capacity		2,433 c.c.	Brake drum diameter	11 in.
Piston area		42.4 sq. in.		
Valves		Overhead (push-rod)	Friction lining area	184 sq. in.
Compression ratio		7.75	Suspension: Front	Independent (laminated torsion bars)
Engine performance				
Max. b.h.p.		100	Rear	Semi-elliptic
at		4,400 r.p.m.	Shock absorbers	Girling telescopic DAS
Max. b.m.e.p.		132 lb./sq. in.		
at		2,500 r.p.m.	Wheel type	Disc
B.h.p. per sq. in. piston area		2.36	Tyre size	6.70 × 15
Peak piston speed ft. per min.		2,570	Steering gear	Bishop cam
			Steering wheel	18-in. spring spoke
Engine details				
Carburetter		Two S.U. H6 (horizontal)	**Dimensions**	
			Wheelbase	8 ft. 8 in.
Ignition		Coil	Track: Front	4 ft. 4 in.
Plugs: make and type		Lodge HLN	Rear	4 ft. 4 in.
Fuel pump		AC Mechanical	Overall length	14 ft. 10¼ in.
Fuel capacity		15 gallons	Overall width	5 ft. 6 in.
Oil filter		Tecalemit full-flow	Overall height	5 ft. 5 in.
Oil capacity		10 pints	Ground clearance	7 in.
Cooling system		Pump, fan and thermostat	Turning circle	34 ft.
			Dry weight	27½ cwt.
Water capacity		18 pints		
Electrical system		12-volt	**Performance data**	
Battery capacity		51 amp./hr.	Piston area, sq. in. per ton	30.8
Transmission			Brake lining area, sq. in. per ton	134
Clutch		Daimler fluid flywheel and pre-selector transmission.	Top gear m.p.h. per 1000 r.p.m.	17.4
Gear ratios: Top		4.56	Top gear m.p.h. at 2,500 ft./min. piston speed	75.0
3rd		6.71		
2nd		10.05		
1st		17.47	Litres per ton-mile dry	3,060
Rev.		23.7		
Prop. shaft		Hardy Spicer, open		
Final drive		Hypoid bevel		

COACHWORK SURVEY (Manufacturer's figures)

Interior length			
(a) Facia panel to rear squab	72 in.	(k) Cushion depth, front to rear	19 in.
Front seat		(l) Total length (j) + (k)	34 in.
(b) Overall width	51 in.	(m) Seat height above floor	16 in.
(c) Brake pedal to edge of seat	16 in.	(n) Headroom above seat	35½ in.
(d) Cushion depth, front to rear	19 in.	(o) Total height (m) + (n)	51½ in.
(e) Total length (c) + (d)	35 in.	**Doors**	
(f) Seat height above floor	14 in.	(p) Front door width, min./max.	30/33 in.
(g) Headroom above seat	35 in.	(q) Rear door width, min./max.	17/24½ in.
(h) Total height (f) + (g)	49 in.	**Windscreen**	
Rear seat		(r) Width between pillars	45 in.
(i) Min. width of seat	43 in.	(s) Height at centre	15½ in.
(j) Knee room	15 in.		

fit the occupants' backs, thereby lessening the fatigue of the driver on long runs and preventing his passenger from being slung sideways against him on fast bends. Both front and rear seats have also been given even greater comfort by the addition of foam rubber cushions beneath the upholstery. Extra equipment fitted as standard to the Century also includes that invaluable modern accessory, the windscreen washer.

Equipment for the rear-seat passengers now includes spring-loaded pull-straps which spring up into the roof when released and an interior light switch mounted on one of the door pillars instead of on the light itself.

An attractive feature of the Century's standard equipment is the provision without extra charge of two suit-cases, one lined and equipped to suit a lady and the other a gentleman, which have been specially designed to make the best possible use of the space in the boot without, however, filling it completely. Even when the cases are being carried, therefore, plenty of space is still available for all those unpackable oddments which usually are stowed loose in the boot.

It is the attention paid to such small but important details as this that make the new Conquest Century a car which will appeal greatly to the experienced motorist.

NEW CARS DESCRIBED

CONQUEST CENTURY

Supplementary Daimler Model Gives Enhanced Performance and Comfort

ALTHOUGH the basic components used in both the Daimler Conquest and the new Conquest Century are similar, a large number of features have been modified to improve both performance and comfort of the latter. The power output from the engine has been increased by 33⅓ per cent, the brakes have been made half an inch wider, and the rear seat has been moved farther back to give increased leg room for the rear passengers. Obtaining an extra 25 b.h.p. from a 2½-litre engine (it now develops 100 b.h.p. at 4,400 r.p.m. compared with 75 b.h.p. at 4,000 r.p.m.) is no mean feat, particularly as it has been done—as the Road Test on the preceding pages shows—without a noticeable loss of smoothness and without redesigning any of the components such as pistons, connecting rods, bearings, and so on.

To obtain this improved performance the engine has been provided with a new light alloy cylinder head which increases the compression ratio from 6.6 to 7.75 to 1. The diameter of the inlet and exhaust valves has been increased by ⅛in to 1 7/16in and 1 5/16in respectively, and a new high-lift camshaft has been substituted, giving a maximum lift at the valves of 0.392in, compared with 0.367in for the standard Conquest engine. The valve timing has also been modified so that the inlet valve opens 13 deg before top dead

The instruments are grouped neatly in the centre section of the polished hardwood facia panel. The rectangular space in the centre of the facia is used to house the radio control unit when fitted.

centre and closes 65 deg after bottom dead centre, while the exhaust valve opens 55 deg before bottom dead centre and closes 23 deg after top dead centre. In the standard Conquest engine the inlet valve opens 17 deg before t.d.c. and closes 55 deg after b.d.c., while the exhaust valve opens 50 deg before b.d.c. and closes 22 deg after t.d.c. The inlet and exhaust ports have also been enlarged, with the result that the gas speeds at the valve throat are 44.43ft per sec inlet and 53.9ft per sec exhaust, compared with 53.9ft per sec inlet and 73.9ft per sec exhaust for the normal engine; all figures are for an engine speed of 1,000 r.p.m. These figures indicate how the r.p.m. figure for optimum gas speeds has been raised. A new inlet manifold is attached to the head and the Conquest Century is fitted with twin sidedraught S.U. carburettors in place of a single downdraught Zenith.

Rally Lessons

As a result of experience gained in the Monte Carlo Rally, modifications have been made to the valve seat inserts and a high thermal expansion steel is now used. Besides improvement of the breathing, modifications have been made to exhaust the gases more efficiently. Twin exhaust manifolds are used, and a straight-through silencer. Other mechanical modifications include the provision of a tachometer drive, and a larger diameter propeller-shaft (2¾in in place of 2¼in).

To enable full benefit to be gained from the improved performance obtained from the increased output of the Century engine, the brake lining area has been increased and the car now has a figure of 117 sq in per ton laden compared with 89.5 sq in on the normal Conquest model.

Although it is sometimes necessary to reduce passenger comfort to obtain improved performance, the reverse applies with the Conquest Century. By

Modifications to the engine include twin exhaust manifolds and a new water-heated inlet manifold to suit the twin S.U. carburettors.

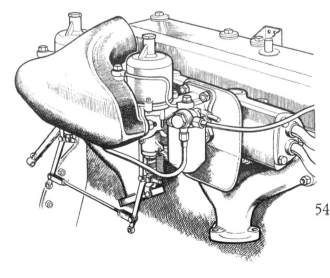

the repositioning of the rear seats an extra four inches of leg room have been obtained in the rear compartment, although this is at the expense of a slight reduction in luggage locker capacity.

Leather-covered foam rubber upholstery is used for all the seats, and the quality of the interior generally is very high. Many useful fittings are included in the standard specification, such as screen wash equipment, fog lights, and two suitcases.

SPECIFICATION

Engine.—6 cyl, 76.2 × 88.9 mm (2,433 c.c.). Compression ratio 7.75 to 1. Four-bearing crankshaft. Side camshaft operating overhead valves by push-rods and rockers. Tecalemit full-flow oil filter.

Transmission.—Daimler fluid flywheel and pre-selector gear box. 4 forward speeds. Overall ratios: Top 4.56, third 6.71, second 10.05, first 17.47 to 1; reverse 23.7 to 1. Open propeller-shaft to hypoid rear axle with four-pinion differential, ratio 4.56 to 1 (9:41).

Suspension.—Independent front by laminated torsion bars and wishbones with Girling telescopic dampers. Front anti-roll bar. Half-elliptic rear with telescopic dampers. Suspension rate (at the wheel): front, 85 lb per in; rear, 114 lb per in.

Brakes.—Girling Hydro-mechanical, with two-leading shoes at front. Drum diameter, 11in front and rear. Drum width, 2¼in front and rear. Total lining area, 95 sq in front; 89 sq in rear.

Steering.—Cam and roller; 18 to 1 ratio at gear.

Wheels and Tyres.—Dunlop 6.70-15in on five-stud steel disc wheels.

Electrical Equipment.—12-volt; 51 ampère-hour battery. Head lamps: double-dip; 42-36 watt bulbs.

Fuel System.—15-gallon tank.

Main Dimensions.—Wheelbase 8ft 8in. Track (front and rear) 4ft 4in. Overall length 14ft 10¾in. Height (unladen) 5ft 5in. Width 5ft 6in. Ground clearance 7in. Turning circle 34ft. Frontal area 22.3 sq ft. Weight (in running trim with 5 gallons of fuel), 27¾ cwt.

Price.—£1,172, plus purchase tax in Great Britain £489 9s 2d. Total £1,661 9s 2d.

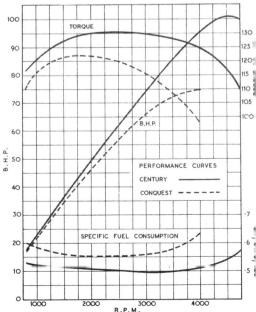

Front and rear doors are hinged at their leading edges and have push-button locks. The left side front door can be locked with the ignition key, which is also needed to unlock the fuel filler cap and serves for the luggage locker lid.

Twin rear lights are built into the wing pressings and a central lamp unit provides the reversing light and number plate illumination.

The Autocar ROAD TESTS

No. 1524

DAIMLER CONQUEST CENTURY SALOON

SOME months ago *The Autocar* was invited to sample a car that looked the same as the normal Daimler Conquest saloon introduced almost a year ago, but was rather special as regards the engine compartment. At the time of its announcement the Conquest saloon was one of the liveliest cars ever to come from the Daimler works—a luxury model with a 2½-litre six-cylinder engine, and giving a mean speed of just over 80 m.p.h. Development work

A traditional Daimler radiator grille blends well with the modern body. Built-in side lights are placed below the head lamps, and twin fog lights quite high on either side of the radiator grille. The bumper over-riders are mounted fairly close together. There is a hole in the bumper for the starting handle.

which has taken place on the power unit has enabled the output to be increased from 75 to 100 b.h.p., a very useful gain, and impressions obtained earlier with the prototype car left little doubt in the minds of those who drove it that the new model—to be called the Conquest Century—would be a car that had really got something. On page 313 of this issue is a description of the model.

It should not be thought that after first designing the Conquest as a luxury saloon the Daimler company have now abandoned the luxury features and converted the model into a new sports saloon, for although performance has been considerably improved, as a glance at the tables will show, the standard of comfort has also been improved. And by modifying the position of the rear seat a considerable increase in rear passenger space has been made, this compartment now being almost as large as that of the Daimler Consort.

In spite of the increase in engine performance, the power unit has not suffered as regards smoothness and flexibility, and both these qualities are of a very high order. Compared with the Conquest, the Century has a slight reduction in the amount of understeer, whilst the fuel consumption is a little heavier if the car is driven fast. The Century is a car that covers the ground very quickly without needing to be driven really fast—this impression was perhaps emphasized by the very accurate speedometer of the car tested. It will cruise very pleasantly at 60, while under favourable road conditions it can maintain at least 70 m.p.h. for very long periods, still having a reserve of 17 or 18 m.p.h. in hand, although the car requires at least two miles of straight to attain its ultimate maximum.

Like all Daimler models, the Century is fitted with a fluid flywheel; this is used in conjunction with a four-speed and reverse preselector gear box. This transmission, combined with the general smoothness of the six-cylinder engine, results in a particularly smooth and pleasant drive, as a

ROAD TEST . . . . continued

demonstration of which the car can be accelerated from rest on a level road in top gear. The gears are preselected by a lever mounted on a steering column quadrant, the actual gear changing being performed by the selection pedal. On the car tested the system was adjusted to give a fairly brisk take-up on the gear box bands in the interests of performance, yet there was still a smooth take-up for normal driving. This arrangement enables the car to be accelerated from rest very smartly, as the performance figures show. The familiar transmission noise of this system, which can best be described as a "quiet growl," is noticed in neutral, and there is a little gear noise in the indirect ratios, but this is not excessive and the remainder of the transmission and the engine are quiet.

Suspension and Steering

The front suspension is unusual in that laminated torsion bars are employed in conjunction with the normal arrangement of wishbones. There is a conventional open propellershaft drive with half-elliptic springs controlled by telescopic dampers. This arrangement results in a very comfortable ride in both front and rear seats over all normal types of road surface, and although, compared with the Conquest, the rear seat of the Century has been moved farther back, it is still just inside the wheelbase. There is very little roll on corners and the roadholding qualities generally are very good. For fast cornering, even with only two persons on board, the handling qualities seem to be improved if the rear tyre pressures are increased to 26 lb per sq in, as at the standard setting of 24 lb all round the car had little or no understeer characteristic. With the slightly harder rear tyres the car corners well and handles very nicely.

The steering is accurate and has a nice feel as well as good self-centring action. A very slight amount of vibration can be felt through the wheel. For a car of this size the turning circle is compact and the Century can be easily manœuvred in confined spaces. Because of the fluid flywheel, the technique for this operation is a little different from normal; for example, when reversing out of a garage in the morning, when the car is cold, it is necessary to check a slight tendency to creep by applying the brakes and releasing · them slightly to "inch back"—a method that is altogether

preferable to the unauthorized method of slipping the reverse brake band by operating the gear change pedal.

In keeping with the increased power output, the brake lining area has been increased compared with that of the existing Conquest saloon. The Century has very powerful brakes, well able to provide rapid retardation from high speed. They are hydraulically operated at the front and mechanically operated at the rear, and on the car tested this system provided well-balanced braking. No fade was experienced either on the road or during the performance testing, and the pedal ratio is just about right to give a nice feel for normal check braking.

Considered with the general character of the car, the Century is a quiet car to drive and ride in. Apart from some transmission noise as mentioned previously, the car is very quiet mechanically; there is a certain amount of road-excited noise, for example, a regular "bump, bump" when the wheels pass over regularly spaced objects such as cat'seyes or joints in the road surface. The body is well insulated from vibration and there is no noticeable body boom. With all windows closed there is very little wind noise and the car is noticeably quiet in the low and medium speed range when the front ventilating panels or side windows are slightly open. There is noticeable noise from the heater unit when the fan is rotating at full speed.

Driving Position

As well as the normal fore-and-aft adjustment for the driving seat, the steering wheel has a useful range of adjustment on its telescopic column and its position can be quickly altered by means of a cam locking device. The combination of these two adjustments caters for the requirements of a very wide variety of drivers. The pedals are also well positioned in relation to both the seat and the steering wheel, and the positions of the brake and throttle pedals permit the use of a heel-and-toe technique. The throttle pedal is placed well towards the right-hand side of the toe board in a very comfortable position; to some tastes, left foot comfort is not quite so well arranged, particularly for night driving in regard to operation of the dip switch at frequent intervals. This control projects rather too far out from the gear box cover and it would be

The interior of the Century is very well trimmed in leather and polished hardwood. All the doors are provided with pockets and have combined pulls and arm rests. There is also a folding central arm rest in the rear seat. Ashtrays are recessed into the front doors and the backs of the front seats. The sides of the floor carpet are fitted into a neat moulded rubber strip.

better if it were moved a little to the right and placed on the toe board to form a rest for the driver's left foot; however, with the present arrangement, such a modification might require an alteration to the gear change pedal position. The hand brake is effective and the pull and push control is conveniently placed to the right of the steering column. It is necessary to pull the handle slightly as well as press the trigger in order to release the brake.

The driver sits comparatively high off the floor, an arrangement that is not only comfortable but also assists vision. There is very good forward visibility and both front wings can be seen, together with the top of the familiar fluted radiator grille. The windscreen pillars are slender and do not restrict vision or cause serious blind spots. The driving mirror is small, so it does not blank an important area of the windscreen, and it is well posi-

tioned in relation to the rear window; it has a useful range and provides a satisfactory rearward view, but, in the absence of a rear window blind, is not of the non-dazzling variety for night use. The screenwipers sweep a wide area of the curved screen and the areas covered by the blades overlap in the centre to form a clear area; they are not self-parking.

All the instruments are placed in the central portion of the polished hardwood facia. Owing to the angle of the dials—which presumably is arranged to prevent reflection in the windscreen at night—it is a little difficult to read the speedometer accurately from a normal driving position; also the centre of the speedometer needle tends to mask the trip mileage recorder. Between the large circular dials of the tachometer and the speedometer four other instruments are grouped; these are a fuel gauge, ammeter, clock

DAIMLER CONQUEST CENTURY SALOON

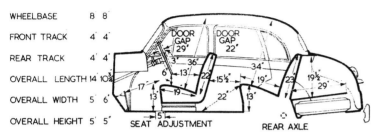

WHEELBASE	8' 8"
FRONT TRACK	4' 4"
REAR TRACK	4' 4"
OVERALL LENGTH	14' 10¾"
OVERALL WIDTH	5' 6"
OVERALL HEIGHT	5' 5"

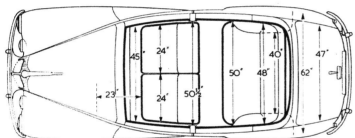

Measurements in these ⅛in to 1ft scale body diagrams are taken with the driving seat in the central position of fore and aft adjustment and with the seat cushions uncompressed.

DATA

PRICE (basic), with saloon body, £1,172.
British purchase tax, £489 9s 2d.
Total (in Great Britain), £1,661 9s 2d.
Extras : Radio £51 4s 1d.
Heater, standard fitting.

ENGINE : Capacity : 2,433 c.c. (148.4 cu in).
Number of cylinders : 6.
Bore and stroke : 76.2 × 88.9 mm (3.0 × 3.5in).
Valve gear : Overhead ; pushrods and rockers.
Compression ratio : 7.75 to 1.
B.H.P. : 100 at 4,400 r.p.m. (B.H.P. per ton laden 63.7).
Torque : 130 lb ft at 2,500 r.p.m.
M.P.H. per 1,000 r.p.m. on top gear, 17.4.

WEIGHT : (with 5 gals fuel), 27¾ cwt (3,117 lb).
Weight distribution (per cent) : F, 50.8 ; R, 49.2.
Laden as tested : 31½ cwt (3,517 lb).
Lb per c.c. (laden) : 1.44.

BRAKES : Type : F, two-leading shoe ; R, leading and trailing.
Method of operation : F, Hydraulic ; R, Mechanical.
Drum dimensions : F, 11in diameter, 2¼in wide. R, 11in diameter, 2¼in wide.
Lining area : F, 95 sq in. R, 89 sq in. (117 sq in per ton laden).

TYRES : 6.70-15in.
Pressures (lb per sq in) : F, 24 ; R, 25 (normal).

TANK CAPACITY : 15 Imperial gallons (including 1½ gallons reserve).
Oil sump, 10 pints.
Cooling system, 18 pints

TURNING CIRCLE : 34ft 0in (L and R).
Steering wheel turns (lock to lock) : 3¼.

DIMENSIONS : Wheelbase : 8ft 8in.
Track : F, 4ft 4in. ; R, 4ft 4in.
Length (overall) : 14ft 10¾in.
Height : 5ft 5in.
Width : 5ft 6in.
Ground clearance : 7in.
Frontal area : 22.3 sq ft (approximately).

ELECTRICAL SYSTEM : 12-volt ; 51 ampère-hour battery.
Head lights : Double dip ; 42-36 watt bulbs.

SUSPENSION : Front, Independent ; wishbones and torsion bars ; anti-roll bar. Rear, Half-elliptic springs.

PERFORMANCE

ACCELERATION : from constant speeds. Speed Range, Gear Ratios and Time in sec.

M.P.H.	4.56 to 1	6.71 to 1	10.05 to 1	17.47 to 1
10—30	9.5	6.6	4.8	—
20—40	9.7	6.6	5.6	—
30—50	10.3	7.2	—	—
40—60	11.6	9.2	—	—
50—70	13.9	—	—	—
60—80	20.6	—	—	—

From rest through gears to :

M.P.H.				sec
30	..	..	..	4.8
50	..	..	..	11.4
60	..	..	..	16.3
70	..	..	..	24.1
80	..	..	..	38.5

Standing quarter mile, 20.7 sec.

SPEEDS ON GEARS :

Gear		M.P.H. (normal and max.)	K.P.H. (normal and max.)
Top	(mean)	87	140.0
	(best)	88	141.6
3rd	.. ..	50—60	80—97
2nd	.. ..	30—41	48—66
1st	.. ..	15—20	24—32

TRACTIVE RESISTANCE : 27.5 lb per ton at 10 M.P.H.

TRACTIVE EFFORT :

	Pull (lb per ton)	Equivalent Gradient
Top	250	1 in 8.9
Third	345	1 in 6.4
Second	450	1 in 4.9

BRAKES :

Efficiency	Pedal Pressure (lb)
89 per cent	80
76 per cent	60
58 per cent	40

FUEL CONSUMPTION :
18.8 m.p.g. overall for 270 miles. (15.0 litres per 100 km.)
Approximate normal range 18-21 m.p.g. (15.7-13.5 litres per 100 km.)
Fuel, First grade.

WEATHER : Dry ; damp surface ; wind negligible.
Air temperature 41 deg F.
Acceleration figures are the means of several runs in opposite directions.
Tractive effort and resistance obtained by Tapley meter.
Model described in *The Autocar* of March 5, 1954.

SPEEDOMETER CORRECTION : M.P.H.

Car speedometer :	.. .. ..	10	20	30	40	50	60	70	80	88
True speed :	.. .. ..	10	20.5	30.5	40	50	60	70	80	88

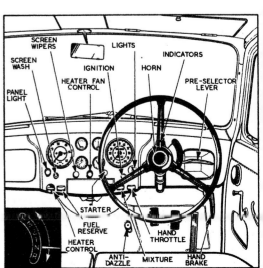

and water temperature gauge. Warning lights indicate low oil pressure, main head light beam, and the use of direction indicators. A rheostat control is provided to vary the intensity of the instrument lighting—it would be even better if this lighting could be further reduced. All the minor controls and switches are grouped below the instruments; these include a valuable reserve petrol control, hand throttle and screen wash control, while an extra position on the light switch switches off the head lamps and brings the fog lamps into operation.

Interior Comfort

Wide doors provide easy access, both front and rear. The separate front seats are of generous proportions, well upholstered and very nicely sprung. The cushions give ample support to the legs and the backs of the seats are more nearly vertical than often applies and shaped to reduce sideways movement during fast cornering. There is also ample head room. The rear seat, too, is well proportioned and there is generous leg room even when the front seats are well back. As well as a pocket in each of the four doors, there are a lockable compartment in the facia, on the passenger's side, and an open locker to the right of the steering column. Flush-fitting sun vizors are provided for both the driver and the front passenger. It would be better if they did not mask quite so much of the windscreen when being used.

The luggage locker is quite roomy ; it is of a useful shape and has a smooth interior. Straps are provided to hold the two suitcases which are standard equipment on this model. A separate lower compartment houses the spare wheel, jack and tools.

ROAD TEST . . . . continued

There is little wasted space in the engine compartment. A large air cleaner and silencer for the intakes of the twin S.U. carburettors is placed to the side of the engine. The dipstick handle can be seen close to the ignition distributor cables. The heater unit is built into the bulkhead behind the engine, and the container for the windscreen wash is placed in front of the brake fluid reservoir. Just behind the radiator, and by the side of the front carburettor, is the automatic chassis lubrication reservoir. When open the bonnet is self-supporting by spring balance mechanism.

An interior light is mounted in the centre of the roof, and although light switches operated by opening the doors are not provided, switches are placed on the inside body pillar between the doors on both sides, so it is possible to switch on the light before getting into the car at night. The heating and ventilating system proved effective both for warming the interior and for demisting the windscreen. Trap doors in the fresh air form of heater unit below the facia control the distribution inside the car. A very worthwhile detail is the use of a glass deflector strip for the front windows. This is placed inside the window at the rear edge of the door, and it virtually eliminates draughts that would otherwise occur when the front side windows are open.

The desire to provide a car that is fully equipped and does not need a large number of accessories to be added by an owner has resulted in the inclusion of two suitcases as part of the standard equipment. These fit neatly into the luggage locker. The 15-gallon fuel tank provides a very useful range; it can be filled quickly without the risk of petrol blowing back.

Ease of Maintenance

This car's head lights are particularly good—the main beam position provides adequate illumination for fast driving, and there is a satisfactory dipped beam. The horns are powerful and have a pleasing note.

For the owner-driver, maintenance is reduced to a minimum by the use of automatic chassis lubrication, and instead of greasing a large number of individual chassis points it is necessary only to top up a tank in the engine compartment. Chassis bearings not covered by the system have rubber bushes. There are three nipples on the propeller-shaft that require lubrication at intervals of 1,000 miles. The battery is located below the rear seat and it is necessary to remove the cushion and a cover in order to check the level in the cells. A starting handle is provided and there are jacking points at front and rear.

The Daimler Conquest Century is a car traditional in character and built to a very high standard of quality and detail finish. It provides very comfortable transport for four, while it is possible to carry a third person on the rear seat on occasion. This car has a fine performance yet it is versatile and is equally suitable for high-speed touring or as a smart town carriage.

The dashing Daimler CONQUEST

IS THE ONLY CAR WITH

* ✳ **fluid transmission**
* ✳ **preselector gearchange**
* ✳ **and automatic chassis lubrication**

No wonder the Daimler 'Conquest' is such a breath-taking car to drive, so lively yet so amazingly easy to handle, so efficient and trouble-free. The famous Daimler fluid flywheel and preselector gearchange provide the smoothest transmission imaginable. The exclusive Automatic Chassis Lubrication, thermostatically controlled, services all the main lubrication points every time the engine warms up. Here are other features which make the 'Conquest' such a desirable car: 6 cylinder O.H.V. engine—75 b.h.p. Petrol consumption from 26.5 m.p.g. at 30 to 21 m.p.g. at 60. 11″ brakes with surface of 148 sq. ins. Independent front suspension with *laminated* torsion bars. Price £1066 plus £445.5.10 p/t.

Make an appointment today for a trial run

HOOPER

HOOPER AND COMPANY (COACHBUILDERS) LIMITED

54 ST. JAMES'S STREET, PICCADILLY, LONDON, SW1. TELEPHONE HYDE PARK 3242

OFFICIAL RETAILERS OF DAIMLER, ROLLS-ROYCE AND BENTLEY · DISTRIBUTORS OF LANCHESTER CARS

60

D232

Two outstanding cars...

THAT ARE BRINGING OWNERS A NEW

AND THRILLING ASPECT OF MOTORING

For detailed brochures on either of these exciting models and the address of your nearest dealer, write today to Bureau 2, The Daimler Company Ltd, Coventry.

by Daimler

BY APPOINTMENT
The Daimler Co. Limited, Motor Car
Manufacturers to the late King George VI

Have you driven the Conquest or the 'Conquest Century' yet? If not, you are missing a really memorable experience. Acceleration is breathtaking. Handling, thanks to preselector fluid transmission, is the easiest you've ever known. Note how these cars corner—no roll, no sway—that's *laminated* torsion bar suspension. What you'll notice later on is the economy achieved by automatic chassis lubrication and that great petrol-saving feature—water-heated induction.

CONQUEST Saloon

The 6-cylinder O.H.V. engine develops 75 b.h.p. Over 80 m.p.h. Acceleration 0-60 in 20.4 secs. through the gears, and 10-30 in 9.7 secs. in top. Petrol from 26.5 m.p.g. at 30 to 21 m.p.g. at 60 (*Autocar & Motor* road test reports). Price £1066 plus £445.5.10 purchase tax.

'CONQUEST CENTURY'

The 'Century' has a special series 100 b.h.p. engine with twin carburettors. Acceleration is remarkable—60 from a standing start in 16.3 secs.! Other modifications include bigger brakes; new instrument panel with rev. counter; telescopic adjustable steering; improved seating and more leg room in rear; foam rubber upholstery; two suitcases specially designed to fit large luggage boot and included in the basic price of £1172 plus £489.9.2 purchase tax.

'OUT OF PEDIGREE
COMES PACE'

One car or three?

THE 100 BHP
DAIMLER CONQUEST *Coupé*

A FAST open tourer with a magnificent perform-ance — a smart 'de ville' with elegance and dignity — a snug closed car with the warmth and comfort of a saloon: not three different cars, but one — the Daimler Conquest Coupé!

POWER-OPERATED DROP-HEAD

This special version of the famous Conquest is amazingly versatile; the powered drop-head, oper-ated by a button under the dash, is adjustable to three positions — open, 'de ville' or closed — in a matter of seconds, with the minimum handling.

SPEED, COMFORT, DIGNITY

The power unit is the 100 bhp Century engine which gives the car quite spectacular acceleration and a top speed of well over 90. Big powerful brakes with a positive yet smoothly progressive action match the high performance. Extra driving comfort is ensured by a telescopic adjustable steering column, and a heater is fitted as standard.

Other notable features of the Conquest Coupé are Daimler preselector fluid transmission, automatic chassis lubrication and really magnificent road hold-ing. The price of this clever com-bination of dash, dignity and com-fort is £1736 . 10 . 10 including purchase tax.

BY *APPOINTMENT*
Motor Car Manufacturers
to the late King George VI

THE DAIMLER COMPANY LIMITED · G.P.O. BOX NO. 29 · RADFORD WORKS · COVENTRY

The DAIMLER Conquest Coupé

A Fast Touring Convertible with Power-operated Hood

WHEN, thirteen months ago, the Daimler Company introduced its new 2.4-litre Conquest saloon, fresh ground was broken by a concern most of whose products, as was freely admitted, had previously been known for staid dignity rather than lively performance. At Earls Court last year the Conquest was accompanied on the Daimler stand by a roadster of imaginative appearance powered by a twin-carburetter, high-compression version of the same engine, developing 100 b.h.p., and in the spring of 1954 the Conquest Century models were announced to the public, being the saloon and a coupé on the same chassis

WINTER AND SUMMER conditions were included within this test, the snowy scene above being on the Mont Cénis Pass in December whilst on the left a later production car is seen in summer motoring trim.

with the more powerful engine. Thus in the course of a year the car which is the subject of the present report has made a considerable departure in several respects from Daimler tradition.

With some justification we claim a more than usually extensive acquaintance with the drophead coupé, the prototype of which was used to carry two members of our staff on a 1,500-odd-mile round trip to Italy some months ago, while a recent weekend of revision enabled us to make some interesting comparisons with the model now in production. The most notable of the differences observed was a reduction in unladen weight of almost two hundredweight, of which the greater part had been taken off the rear axle with a small effect on front/rear weight distribution. Reference will be made to this in consideration of the performance figures obtained with the prototype; for the moment some more general comments may be made on a car in which performance is still, perhaps, not the prime consideration.

Fairly well up in the price range, the Conquest coupé is intended for a well-defined market amongst those who require

comfortable, long-distance motoring and in particular a truly convertible four-seater. In the last respect it is rare among current British productions in the provision of a power-operated hood which, a small detail in itself, is the key to the character of the car.

With a width between the front arm rests of 44½ in., and 40 in. between those at the back, the Daimler lays claim to

In Brief

Price: £1,225 plus purchase tax £511 10s. 10d., equals £1,736 10s. 10d.
Capacity ... ... 2,433 c.c.
Unladen kerb weight:
  Model tested ... ... 29½ cwt.
  Later production ... 27¾ cwt.
Fuel consumption... ... 19.7 m.p.g.
Maximum speed ... ... 89.0 m.p.h.
Maximum speed on 1 in 20
  gradient ... ... 75 m.p.h.
Maximum top gear gradient 1 in 8.4
Acceleration:
  10-30 m.p.h. in top ... 9.7 sec.
  0-50 m.p.h. through gears 13.5 sec.
Gearing: 17.4 m.p.h. in top at 1,000 r.p.m.; 74.5 m.p.h. at 2,500 ft. per minute piston speed.

seating only four people in the standard of comfort associated with this class of motoring, although the almost flat floor and the "bench" shape of the separate front seats make another passenger just possible for short runs. One might in fact wish that the seats had their squabs curved to give more lateral support; in every other respect, however, they are excellent, deeply upholstered to provide an untiring ride for driver and passengers, and upright enough to give the former a really commanding position for his work. This is a high-built car, in which not only the floor line but the seats are high, so that there is none of the "cushion-on-the-floor" effect often found in fast touring machines. A high bonnet obscuring the near-side front wing is the only disappointing factor in the view ahead through a fixed windscreen with substantial but reasonably slim pillars.

A change from the prototype is that the side windows are now raised and lowered manually, those in the doors having quite quick-acting handles (working contrary to the usual direction, so that winding them forwards raises the glass), while the quarter lights are pivoted but without handles and must be swung down into the body by taking hold of the frame. As there are no body side pillars this is more easily done with the front windows lowered.

Operation of the hood, which can be moved manually if necessary after turning a release handle behind the driver's seat, is extremely simply effected from a button

VISION outwards from the rear seat is good even with the power-operated roof raised, thanks to the provision of opening quarter lights to the rear of the large doors.

The Daimler Conquest Coupé - -

moval of surplus weight since our tests on the prototype car will have brought some improvement in the acceleration figures. The maximum speed (measured with hood and windows raised) is unlikely to be much altered at just short of 90 m.p.h., nor should there be any difference in the figures for fuel consumption at steady speeds, which are taken on a more or less level road. A 200-mile check on overall consumption with the later car also indicated substantially the same figure of 19.7 m.p.g.

Supplementary Throttle

Pleasantly docile despite its good specific output, the engine is not quite a first-touch starter, but warms up quickly with some temporary use of the choke. A pull-out hand throttle is provided which is useful to set a fairly fast tick-over, necessary to avoid slightly uneven slow running, but which makes the car inclined to creep when in gear, unless it is held with the brakes. This control has another use in conjunction with the pre-selector epicyclic gearbox and the Daimler fluid flywheel, which have been features of cars from this concern for many years past. For easy manoeuvring in a confined space, and more particularly on a hill, the technique can be adopted of setting the engine to run at about 1,500 r.p.m., sufficient to provide all the power required, and driving the car solely on the brake pedal. Readers familiar with certain cars equipped with this transmission in the recent past will observe that the arrangement is more "fluid" than that sometimes used, a higher engine speed being needed for positive engagement under load. While power losses are inevitable under hard acceleration at low speed, this does allow the engine to reach the useful part of its speed range, and at the same time makes for great flexibility; for leisurely driving in flat country it is in fact possible to use top gear only, neglecting the gear-change pedal entirely once the gear is engaged, even for starting from rest. As an interesting comparison, acceleration from 0-30 m.p.h. in top gear

beneath the facia panel, adjacent to the steering column. Before retracting it completely into the well behind the rear seat, the cant rails bracing the front part of the hood must be "broken" in the usual way; alternatively, the remainder of the hood may be left in the "de ville" position, the furled material and rails held up by the straps provided. With hood and windows lowered the only part of the car projecting above the waistline is the windscreen, and incidentally, visibility is much improved in a driving mirror whose range of vision is otherwise severely restricted by the small rear window. With the car completely closed draught-proofing is remarkably good, the small apertures above the window frames being high enough to cause little trouble, and the only serious shortcoming of this body when judged as a two-door saloon is the wind noise which appears to originate in the region of the windscreen pillars. For winter conditions, even the fairly mild ones which accompanied most of our continental journey, a greater output from the heater would be desirable, but this unit earns the fullest marks for taking in really fresh air through an intake on top of the scuttle, clear of traffic fumes.

If we have dwelt at some length on the interior comfort and convenience of the Daimler, it is to emphasize that it is not, and is not intended to be, a sports car; this in spite of the excellent performance put up recently by Conquest Century saloons in both rally and racing events. Its performance nevertheless places it in a category outside the normal run of family cars, open or closed, and it may be reasonably expected that the re-

POLISHED woodwork on the facia panel is a feature expected upon cars of the Daimler class. Use of a pistol-grip handbrake and a steering-column control for the pre-selective transmission leave the front compartment entirely unobstructed.

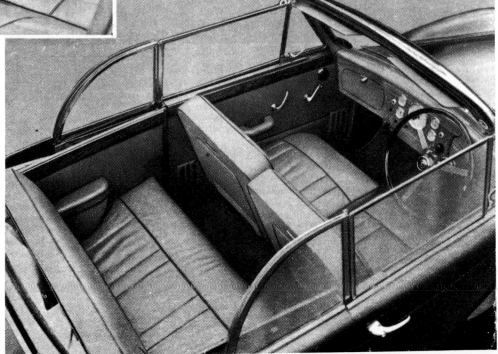

FOUR passengers are comfortably accommodated in pleasing surroundings by the two-door convertible body. Individual front seats upholstered in leather are evident in this picture.

- - - Contd.

SEPARATED from the stowage for the spare wheel and tools, the flat-floored luggage locker is of useful roominess despite encroachment by a well into which the roof folds.

alone takes 14.4 sec., against 6.2 sec. using the gearbox. For fast driving the change is, of course, both quick and crash-proof, and is made literally with the finger-tips, but a routine is needed, especially at night, to ensure that the selector lever is in the intended position in its quadrant before the pedal is pressed. A valuable improvement would be an illuminated pointer on the steering column to indicate the gear selected. An annoying feature of the prototype, which now appears to have been largely eliminated, was vibration of the gear-change pedal at high speeds in the indirect gears, sufficient to restrict the comfortable maximum speed in third to about 50 m.p.h. and thus to have an adverse effect on acceleration. While the vibration on the production model was no longer so severe, it was still present at speed and easily felt through the driver's left foot, which normally rests in close proximity to the pedal. However, a cruising speed of a genuine 75 m.p.h. does not appear to overwork either the car or its occupants.

Stability and Suspension

Firmer than is nowadays customary, the suspension (independent at the front by laminated torsion bars) reacts to bad road surfaces in a manner that is heard rather than felt, thanks largely to the well-padded upholstery, and one has cause to thank the firmness for a lack of pitching when the brakes are applied suddenly. For a car which is high rather than wide there is not an inordinate amount of roll, but as mentioned earlier, more curvature of the seat backs would help to prevent passengers sliding about. Tyres softer than recommended help to cushion the ride for gentle driving, but squeal quite obtrusively if the car is cornered energetically, and for most purposes it is preferable to increase the pressures. Adhesion is quite good on both wet and dry surfaces, the understeer encountered on entering a corner giving way to oversteer if the car is accelerated hard. The steering is light and rather low geared, and there is some lost motion which makes rapid changes of direction difficult. On the car in its production form reaction through the wheel had been reduced, but could still be felt.

Praise must be given to the 11-in. hydro-mechanical brakes which not only produced maximum retardation with light pedal pressure but stood up well to Alpine motoring, showing no signs of fading even on the heavier early model, and for this kind of driving, the easy change-down possible with a pre-selector gearbox is of considerable help. The handbrake, although of pull-out type, requires no great effort to hold the car on a steep hill.

The polished-wood facia panel contains five instruments of unusual and excellent legibility, a large circular speedometer with distance recorder and trip, flanked by ammeter, radiator thermometer, fuel gauge and clock. In addition there is a red warning light for the ignition and a green one to indicate low oil pressure, and minor controls include buttons for the starter and electric wipers—adequate, but not self-parking—heater and panel-light rheostats, a temperature control for the heater and a pull-out knob governing the petrol reserve of about two gallons. A switch conveniently placed near the driver's left hand controls headlights of fair but not outstanding range, fitted with a foot-dipper, and two built-in fog lamps.

Wide pockets in the doors supplement a very small open cubby-hole on the driver's side of the facia and one on the other side not much bigger—it will not, for example, take the car's stiff-backed instruction book—can be locked with the ignition key. The latter also fits the lock of the large and useful luggage boot, in which the spare wheel and tools are carried in a separate tray and are removable without disturbing any other contents.

Occasional Maintenance

One further feature of the Daimler must properly be mentioned, well-suited as it is to a car of just this type. While it is not expected that the owner would contemplate doing his own routine servicing, the temporary loss of a car while this is done can be a nuisance in many circumstances; by virtue of the automatic chassis lubrication system on the Daimler it is possible to go for long periods without any thought of maintenance at all. In point of fact the test car on its return from Italy was taken straight down to Wales and back, adding a further 500 miles to the distance covered, and in the whole of that time was not touched with a tool of any description.

Appealing to the buyer in search of fast and comfortable open-car motoring for four people, yet withall a dual-purpose car which can be as snug as a saloon when required, the Conquest coupé should have a sure future in a category in which it has few competitors.

Mechanical Specification

Engine

Cylinders	6
Bore	76.2 mm.
Stroke	88.9 mm.
Cubic capacity	2,433 c.c.
Piston area	42.4 sq.in.
Valves	Pushrod o.h.v.
Compression ratio	7.75/1
Max. power	100 b.h.p.
at	4,400 r.p.m.
Piston speed at max. b.h.p.	2,566 ft. per min.
Carburetters	2 S.U., type H.6
Ignition	Lucas coil
Sparking plugs	14mm. Lodge HLN
Fuel pump	AC mechanical
Oil filter	Tecalemit

Transmission

Clutch	Daimler fluid flywheel
Gearbox	Pre-selective epicyclic
Top gear	4.56
3rd gear	6.71
2nd gear	10.05
1st gear	17.47
Propeller shaft	Hardy Spicer open (2¾ in. dia.)
Final drive	Hypoid bevel (4-star differential)
Top gear m.p.h. at 1,000 r.p.m.	17.4
Top gear m.p.h. at 1,000 ft./min. piston speed	29.8

Chassis

Brakes	Girling hydro-mechanical
Brake drum diameter	11 in.
Friction lining area	184 sq. in.
Suspension:	
Front	Independent (wishbones and laminated torsion bars)
Rear	Semi-elliptic
Shock absorbers	Girling telescopic
Tyres	Dunlop 6.70—15

Steering

Steering gear	Bishop cam and roller
Turning circle	34 feet
Turns of steering wheel, lock to lock	3¾

Performance factors (at laden weight as tested):

Piston area, sq. in. per ton	25.2
Brake lining area, sq. in. per ton	109
Specific displacement, litres per ton mile	2,485

Fully described (saloon) in *The Motor*, March 10, 1954.

Coachwork and Equipment

Bumper height with car unladen:
Front (max.) 21 in., (min.) 11½ in.
Rear (max.) 23 in., (min.) 14 in.

Starting handle	Yes
Battery mounting	Under rear seat
Jack	Screw type
Jacking points	4 on frame, front and rear

Standard tool kit: Tool roll, 3 d/e spanners, box spanner, tommy bar, hub cap spanner, adjustable spanner, oil plug extractor, pliers, screwdriver, distributor gauge, oil gun, grease gun, jack, wheel brace, brake bleeder tube, hub cover remover.

Exterior lights: 2 headlamps, 2 sidelamps, 2 fog-lamps, 2 stop/tail lamps, number plate lamp, reversing lamp.

Direction indicators	Flashing type self-cancelling
Windscreen wipers	2-blade electric, non-self parking
Sun vizors	Two

Instruments: Speedometer with decimal trip, fuel contents gauge, ammeter, coolant thermometer, clock.

Warning lights: Dynamo charge, oil pressure, direction indicators, headlamp main beam.

Locks:

With ignition key	Doors, luggage locker, glove locker, petrol filler
With other keys	Nil
Glove lockers	2 (small) on facia panel, one with lid and lock
Map pockets	2 on doors

Parcel shelves: Nil (well behind rear seat available for parcels only when folding top is erect)

Ashtrays 4 (2 in doors, 2 behind front seats)

Cigar lighters	Nil
Interior lights	1 on hood frame

Interior heater: Heater and de-mister with fresh air intake on top of scuttle.

Car radio	Optional extra
Extras available	Laminated glass windscreen, radio
Upholstery material	Leather
Floor covering	Rubber-backed carpets

Exterior colours standardized: 5 (black, silver grey, light green, ivory, blue).

Alternative body styles: 4-door 6-light saloon; 2-seat roadster.

The Motor Road Test No. 19/54 (Continental)

Make: Daimler   **Type:** Conquest Coupé (2 carburetters)
Makers: The Daimler Co. Ltd., Coventry

TRACK :- FRONT / REAR 4'- 4"
SEATS ADJUSTABLE
OVERALL WIDTH 5'- 5½"
5'- 2"
GROUND CLEARANCE 7"
8'- 8"
14'- 9"
DAIMLER "CONQUEST COUPE"
SCALE 1:50

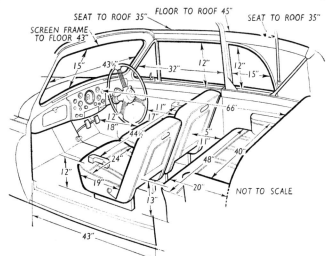

SEAT TO ROOF 35"   FLOOR TO ROOF 45"   SEAT TO ROOF 35"
SCREEN FRAME TO FLOOR 43"
NOT TO SCALE

WEIGHT (see text)
Unladen kerb weight .. .. 29½ cwt.
Front/rear weight distribution .. 51/49
Weight laden as tested .. .. 33¾ cwt.
N.B.—Tests made on early example: Unladen kerb weight of a later car 27¾ cwt.

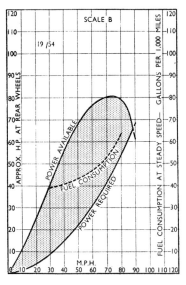

SCALE B
19/54
POWER AVAILABLE
FUEL CONSUMPTION
POWER REQUIRED
APPROX. H.P. AT REAR WHEELS
GALLONS PER 1,000 MILES — FUEL CONSUMPTION AT STEADY SPEED
M.P.H.

Drag at 10 m.p.h. .. .. .. 46 lb.
Drag at 60 m.p.h. .. .. .. 201 lb.
Specific Fuel Consumption when cruising at 80% of maximum speed (i.e. 71.2 m.p.h.) on level road, based on power delivered to rear wheels .. .. 0.72 pints/b.h p./hr.

Test Data

CONDITIONS. *Cold, damp weather with moderate cross wind. Damp concrete road surface (Ostend-Ghent motor road). Premium grade pump fuel. Car tested carrying 2 people and luggage.*

INSTRUMENTS

Speedometer at 30 m.p.h. .. .. 2% fast
Speedometer at 60 m.p.h. .. .. 6% fast
Speedometer at 80 m.p.h. .. .. 4% fast
Distance recorder .. .. 5% fast
(1% fast on later car)

MAXIMUM SPEEDS

Flying Quarter Mile
Mean of Four Opposite Runs .. 89.0 m.p.h.
Best Time equals .. .. 90.5 m.p.h.

Speed in gears
Max. speed in 3rd gear .. .. 61 m.p.h.
Max. speed in 2nd gear .. .. 41 m.p.h.

FUEL CONSUMPTION

25.5 m.p.g. at constant 30 m.p.h.
24.5 m.p.g. at constant 40 m.p.h.
23.0 m.p.g. at constant 50 m.p.h.
21.5 m.p.g. at constant 60 m.p.h.
19.0 m.p.g. at constant 70 m.p.h.
16.0 m.p.g. at constant 80 m.p.h.
Overall consumption for 1384 miles, 70.3 gallons, equals 19.7 m.p.g.
Fuel tank capacity 15 gallons.

ACCELERATION TIMES Through Gears

0-30 m.p.h. .. .. 6.2 sec.
0-40 m.p.h. .. .. 9.2 sec.
0-50 m.p.h. .. .. 13.5 sec.
0-60 m.p.h. .. .. 19.7 sec.
0-70 m.p.h. .. .. 27.7 sec.
0-80 m.p.h. .. .. 39.0 sec.
Standing Quarter Mile .. .. .. 21.4 sec.

ACCELERATION TIMES on Two Upper Ratios

	Top	3rd
10-30 m.p.h.	9.7 sec.	6.5 sec.
20-40 m.p.h.	9.5 sec.	6.6 sec.
30-50 m.p.h.	9.7 sec.	7.5 sec.
40-60 m.p.h.	11.5 sec.	—
50-70 m.p.h.	14.7 sec.	—
60-80 m.p.h.	19.1 sec.	—

HILL CLIMBING (at steady speeds)

Max. top gear speed on 1 in 20 .. .. .. 75 m.p.h.
Max. top gear speed on 1 in 15 .. .. .. 69 m.p.h.
Max. top gear speed on 1 in 10 .. .. .. 53 m.p.h.
Max. gradient on top gear .. 1 in 8.4 (Tapley 265 lb./ton)
Max. gradient on 3rd gear .. 1 in 5.7 (Tapley 385 lb./ton)

BRAKES at 30 m.p.h.

0.90g retardation .. (= 33⅓ ft. stopping distance) with 75 lb. pedal pressure
0.70g retardation .. (= 43 ft. stopping distance) with 50 lb. pedal pressure
0.25g retardation .. (= 120 ft. stopping distance) with 25 lb. pedal pressure

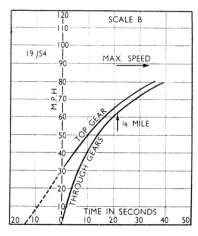

SCALE B
19/54
MAX. SPEED
TOP GEAR
¼ MILE
THROUGH GEARS
M.P.H.
TIME IN SECONDS

Maintenance

Sump: 10 pints, S.A.E. 30. **Fluid flywheel:** 8 pints, S.A.E. 30. **Gearbox:** 5½ pints, S.A.E. 30. **Rear Axle:** 2½ pints, S.A.E. 90 E.P. gear oil. **Steering Gear:** S.A.E. 90 E.P. gear oil. **Radiator:** 18 pints (3 drain taps). **Chassis Lubrication:** By oil gun every 1,000 miles to 3 points on propeller shaft, by grease gun to water pump every 3,000 miles (Automatic lubrication to 15 points). **Ignition Timing:** 9° b.t.d.c. static. **Spark plug gap:** 0.020 in. **Contact breaker gap:** 0.014 in.-0.016 in. **Valve timing:** I.O., 13° b.t.d.c.; I.C., 65° a.b.d.c.; E.O., 55° b.b.d.c.; E.C., 23° a.t.d.c. Tappet clearances (Hot) Inlet and Exhaust, 0.013 in. **Front wheel toe in :** ⅛ in. **Camber Angle :** 1½° **Castor Angle :** zero. **Tyre Pressures:** Front 24 lb. Rear 24-26 lb. according to load. **Brake fluid :** Girling crimson. **Battery :** 12 volt, 51 amp.-hr., Lucas GTW9A. **Lamp bulbs :** 1 volt. Headlamps : 42/36 watt (Lucas No. 354) ; Sidelamps/direction indicators and stop/tail lamps, 18/6 watt (Lucas No. 361). Number plate lamp, 6 watt (Lucas No. 222). Reversing lamp, 18 watt (Lucas No. 221). Fog lamps, 38 watt (Lucas No. 325).

Ref. B/25/54.

D226

POWER – *in a velvet glove*

The Daimler CONQUEST ROADSTER

Here is speed with the accent on luxury—dash with an air of lordly distinction—power in a velvet glove.

The Conquest Roadster has been specially conceived and designed for the kind of motorist who is concerned with something more than mere speed. The driver of the Roadster, while knowing that his car will do a cool 100 when called upon to do so, will enjoy most of all the very real comfort, the spaciousness and the high quality of appointments so unusual in a car of this kind.

The special engine with high compression cylinder head

develops 100 bhp, and has been designed to tuck well down into the chassis to allow for a low over-all height. The hydro-mechanical brakes are cooled by air-vents provided in the body front and rear.

The Roadster is equipped with preselector fluid transmission, automatic chassis lubrication, laminated torsion bar suspension and water-heated induction, those unique Daimler features which contribute so much to the performance, ease of handling and maintenance of all cars in the Conquest range.

For a fully descriptive brochure on the Conquest Roadster write today to Bureau R2, The Daimler Company Ltd, Coventry. Price £1,180 plus £492.15.10 purchase tax.

The Conquest range also includes the Conquest Saloon, the 'Conquest Century' and the Conquest Coupé.

OUT OF PEDIGREE COMES PACE

BY APPOINTMENT *The Daimler Co. Ltd, Motor Car Manufacturers to the late King George VI*

—The Daimler Conquest Roadster

New Open Edition of the 2½-litre Offers Three-figure Maximum, Very Lively Acceleration and Responsive Handling Characteristics

LOW build and smooth contours characterize the Daimler Roadster. The bonnet air intakes serve the practical purposes of ducting cool air to the carburetters and reducing under-bonnet temperature.

In Brief

Price £1,180 plus purchase tax
£492 15s. 10d., equals £1,672 15s. 10d.

Capacity	2,433 c.c.
Unladen kerb weight ...	25½ cwt.
Fuel consumption ...	21.4 m.p.g.
Maximum speed ...	100.7 m.p.h.
Maximum speed on 1 in 20 gradient	91 m.p.h.
Maximum top gear gradient	1 in 8.1

Acceleration:

10-30 m.p.h. in top ...	9.1 sec.
0-50 m.p.h. through gears	10.6 sec.

Gearing: 18.9 m.p.h. in top at 1,000 r.p.m.; 81.2 m.p.h. at 2,500 ft. per min. piston speed.

IN the course of barely a year, the old-established name of Daimler has come to bear a new significance in which performance is accented as well as the traditional Daimler characteristics of quality and sound engineering. The process started in May last year with the introduction of the 80-m.p.h. 2½-litre Conquest. In October, this model was supplemented by a striking Roadster with a special two-carburetter edition of the engine and various other special features,

and, since then, two more variations of the Conquest have appeared in the shape of the Century saloon with a high-efficiency two-carburetter engine, and a four-seater drop-head coupé, also with the special Century engine.

An example of the latter formed the subject of a road test in this journal three weeks ago, and we are now able to supplement this with a test of the Roadster.

This new open model belongs to the still-select group of cars capable of a genuine 100 m.p.h. In this respect the Roadster proved itself a good 10 m.p.h. faster than the more roomy and luxurious coupé, and it is worthy of note that the Roadster is not only 10 m.p.h. faster in maximum speed, but, by an interesting coincidence, is almost exactly that degree ahead in acceleration in the upper ranges. Thus, the coupé reaches 80 m.p.h. from rest in 39 sec., which is within half a second of the time required by the Roadster to reach 90 m.p.h., there being similar parallels at all speeds from 60 m.p.h. upwards. This interesting 10 m.p.h. comparison can be carried even further if the top gear acceleration figures are examined, the 60-80 m.p.h. time of the

coupé, for example, being remarkably close to the 70-90 m.p.h. figure of the Roadster.

Such comparison between the coupé and the Roadster has been deliberately stressed because both offer open motoring, but whereas one provides luxurious and fast travel for four, the other is a two-seater pure and simple with a reduced degree of comfort and a considerably increased degree of performance.

Wide Speed Range

Despite its two carburetters, high-lift cams, high compression and modified timing, however, the Roadster offers very notable fuel economy, reaching the excellent figure of 34½ m.p.g. at a constant 30 m.p.h., and it is not until 80 m.p.h. is exceeded that the consumption drops below 20 m.p.g. Despite the hard driving which a car of this type invariably invites, an overall figure of 21.4 m.p.g. was recorded for the 833 miles over which consumption was checked.

Except in two respects, the Daimler Roadster achieved these results with none of the penalties which are associated in many people's minds with a high efficiency engine. Perhaps its faults had better be disposed of at the outset. They are an exhaust note which is amusing when one is in the mood, but which becomes tiresome on long journeys and, in practice, often discourages full use of the fine performance of the car. Of less importance —and perhaps peculiar to the particular car tried—was a rather irregular tick-over.

In all other respects, the performance of the engine proved very satisfactory. It is smooth and effortless throughout its entire range and rapidly swings the needle of the rev. counter round to the

TWIN rear lamps, reversing lights and flashing direction indicators are built into a fin extending from the rear wings. The large expanse of the luggage boot lid is a noticeable feature of this view of the car.

69

The Daimler Conquest Roadster -

5,000 mark at which a cautionary red line is inscribed. In practice, another 500-600 revs. are obtainable (making 72 m.p.h. possible in third gear), but such engine speeds are neither desirable nor necessary since the unit is remarkably flexible and provides a wide performance overlap on the nicely-spaced gear ratios.

On the open road, the car reaches a genuine 80 m.p.h. quickly and holds it well, gradients of 1 in 15 being easily within its capabilities at this speed.

Thanks to the flexibility of the engine, the Roadster will also trickle along sweetly at 10 m.p.h. in top gear and, if the fluid flywheel is allowed to do its work, will even start from rest in top and accelerate away smoothly and far from sluggishly right up through the entire range to 100 m.p.h. In

this connection, the top-gear acceleration figures are significant, showing an almost exactly constant rate of acceleration from 10 m.p.h. to 50 m.p.h. with very little tailing off above that speed until maximum is approached.

Other virtues of the power unit which may be summarized briefly include easy starting, quick warming-up, adequate cooling even under adverse conditions (performance tests failed to raise the temperature above normal), an entire absence of running-on and mild pinking at low speeds only on some premium grade fuels. Accessibility through the rear-hinged bonnet (provided with two safety catches) is generally good and full marks must be given for a very well-placed dipstick. The two raised air vents in the bonnet top are no mere ornaments; one is ducted direct to the air cleaner intake and the other serves to reduce under-bonnet temperatures.

The Daimler transmission, which

combines a fluid flywheel with an epicyclic preselector gearbox, is too well known to need a description here: what does need emphasizing is the excellent way in which its characteristics harmonize with the sporting qualities of this car, not only enabling very quick changes to be made, but also making it possible for the driver to preselect a desired ratio before entering a corner or negotiating an obstacle and then, by a mere kick of the pedal, achieve the desired change at the exact moment required, leaving both hands free. When stationary in neutral, the usual epicyclic whine is present, but by no means obtrusive, and generally speaking the gears may be regarded as very quiet.

As the figures show, the brakes provided good stopping power with very moderate pedal pressure and they gave every confidence at high speeds. A car of this type, however, does deserve a better handbrake than the simple pistol-grip type tucked away right under the facia.

Precise Steering

The suspension possesses a certain degree of sports-car firmness without being actually harsh, and roadholding is at all times above reproach. Steering and cornering are in every way in keeping with the performance. The steering is fairly high geared but, with the big nicely-placed wheel (with a column adjustment to suit drivers of varying heights), the effort required is moderate and the driver always has the feeling of being able to place the car accurately. Cornering characteristics are devoid of vices and the car can be held in both slow and fast corners in most reassuring fashion.

This feeling of confidence is augmented by major controls which, apart from the handbrake, are well placed, and by minor controls which are readily reached and not liable to confusion.

LARGE enough to accept a considerable amount of luggage, the boot also has recesses at the sides into which odds and ends may be stowed. A trapdoor in the floor gives access to the spare wheel.

THE clean layout of the engine, the accessible dipstick and large air silencer into which air is fed from the intake on the bonnet are notable features of the engine compartment.

- - - - - - Contd.

A further undoubted aid to accurate handling is the excellent view over the front wings and low bonnet. The wing lamps (with their red tips clearly visible at night) can both be seen from the driving seat by even a short driver and the field of vision is wide, thanks to the curved screen, the considerable wrap-round of which causes no noticeable distortion. The view to the side and rear with the hood and side screens in place is also very satisfactory, but one could wish that the seats were a little lower in relation to the top of the screen, particularly when the wipers are in action. A further point about the screen is that its pronounced slope produces irritating reflections of the instruments.

The individually-adjustable seats have high squabs set in an alert position and are shaped to give some lateral support; it would be better, however, were the leading in a special compartment behind the seats, where it is easy to reach but well away from the heat of the engine.

Luggage accommodation is first class. The main area of the boot has a flat floor which will accommodate the largest of suitcases and although there is a step up at the forward end, the increased height of the tail at this point makes a second layer of suitcases possible. There are also very useful and quite sizable recesses in the rear wing which provide ample stowage for tools and oddments. The large boot lid makes access easy and the fact that its hinges are spring-loaded prevents it being cumbersome to open. The spare wheel is carried beneath the main floor of the boot.

So far as the stowage of oddments within the body is concerned, there are two small cubby holes in the facia panel and a pocket in each door. The latter are quite sizable but would hold more if the trim-panels were extended upwards to make them, in effect, deeper. Both with

ADEQUATE rearward vision when the hood and side curtains are erected is permitted by the large rear window. Signalling flaps are provided on both sides.

edges of the cushion provided with some form of roll to give more support to the thighs.

As an open car, the Daimler is pleasant but would be improved by lower seating in relation to the body sides, an alteration which would probably make the interior less susceptible to back draught.

Two-man Hood

With hood and sidescreens erected, the Daimler is particularly snug—almost too much so in fact, because there is no provision for admitting fresh air and when travelling fairly slowly in hot weather it is necessary to prop open one or other of the signalling flaps with an elbow to keep reasonably cool. Some hood rattles were noticeable on Belgian pavé surfaces.

The hood folds down very neatly behind the rear squabs, but the operation of raising and lowering it is a job more easily performed by two people than by one. Captive nuts would be an improvement on the present detachable wing nuts used for securing the side screens. Stowage of the latter is particularly neat, the divided envelope provided for them fitting into a horizontal recess behind the seats. The battery is also neatly accommodated and without the hood erected, there is room for a considerable quantity of odds and ends behind the seat.

As will be gathered from the tabulated data, the facia board is very well equipped, but many sporting drivers would prefer to have the revolution counter in front of them and the speedometer on the passenger's side instead of the opposite arrangement which has been adopted. A useful detail is a grab handle on the facia for the passenger, but a surprising omission is the absence of an ash tray. Another point of criticism is the arrangement of the door handles (internal only) which are awkward to use both from within and without, but particularly so with hood up and side curtains in place.

Good headlamps are of the utmost importance on a high-performance car and this Daimler is fitted with the latest Lucas "Le Mans 24" type which combine range and spread to a most praiseworthy degree. Normal cruising speeds of the car are well within the range of the lamps and 90 m.p.h. proved possible after dark. Supplementing the main headlamps are a long-range auxiliary and a fog lamp, whilst good marks must also be given for a most adequate pair of reversing lights.

Mechanical Specification

Engine

Cylinders	6
Bore	76.2 mm.
Stroke	88.9 mm.
Cubic capacity	2,433 c.c.
Piston area	42.4 sq.in.
Valves	Overhead (push rod)
Compression ratio	7.75/1
Max. power	100 b.h.p.
at	4,400 r.p.m.
Piston speed at max. b.h.p.	2,570 ft. per min.
Carburetter	Two horizontal S.U.
Ignition	12-volt coil
Sparking plugs	Lodge 14 mm. CLN
Fuel pump	AC mechanical
Oil filter	Tecalemit full-flow

Transmission

Clutch	Daimler fluid flywheel and epicyclic pre-selector transmission
Top gear	4.1
3rd gear	6.05
2nd gear	9.05
1st gear	15.7
Propeller shaft	Hardy Spicer, open
Final drive	Hypoid bevel with 4-star differential
Top gear m.p.h. at 1,000 r.p.m.	18.9
Top gear m.p.h. at 1,000 ft./min. piston speed	32.5

Chassis

Brakes	Girling hydro-mechanical
Brake drum diameter	11 in.
Friction lining area	184 sq. in.
Suspension:	
Front	Independent by laminated torsion bars and wishbones
Rear	Semi-elliptic
Shock absorbers:	
Front	Girling telescopic, DAS 5/45
Rear	Girling telescopic, DAS 6/40
Tyres	6.00 x 15 Dunlop Road Speed

Steering

Steering gear	Bishop cam
Turning circle:	
Left	34 feet
Right	34 feet
Turns of steering wheel, lock to lock	2¼

Performance factors (at laden weight as tested)

Piston area, sq. in. per ton	29.2
Brake lining area, sq. in. per ton	127
Specific displacement, litres per ton mile	2,660

Fully described in *The Motor*, October 21, 1953.

Coachwork and Equipment

Bumper height with car unladen:
  Front (max.) 19¾ in., (min.) 10¾ in.
  Rear (max) 21¼ in., (min.) 12¼ in.

Starting handle	Yes
Battery mounting	Behind driver's seat in separate compartment
Jack	Mechanical screw type
Jacking points	4 on chassis, front and rear

Standard tool kit: Foot pump, jack, wheelbrace, grease gun, oil gun (for fluid flywheel), 3 double-ended spanners, box spanner (for plugs), hub-cap spanner, adjustable spanner, flywheel oil-plug extractor, pliers, screwdriver distributor screwdriver and feeler gauge, bleeder equipment (for brakes), hub-cover remover, tool roll and jack bag.

Exterior lights: 2 headlamps (double-dipping), long-range auxiliary lamp, fog lamp, 2 side lights, 2 front indicator lamps, 2 rear stop/tail/indicator lamps, 2 reversing lamps, rear number plate lamp.

Direction indicators	Flasher type, self-cancelling
Windscreen wipers	Dual, electrical
Sun vizors	None

Instruments: Speedometer (with trip), revolution indicator, clock, fuel gauge, ammeter, thermometer.

Warning lights: For oil pressure, ignition, headlamp main beam and direction indicators.

Locks:

With ignition key	Petrol filler and boot
With other keys	None
Glove lockers	Two
Map pockets	Two (in doors)
Parcel shelves	None
Ashtrays	None
Cigar lighters	None
Interior lights	None
Interior heater	None
Car radio	None
Extras available	None
Upholstery material	Leather
Floor covering	Carpeting

Exterior colours standardized: Red, ivory, silver, powder blue.

Alternative body styles: Conquest Century saloon and d.h. 4-str. coupé have chassis similar in many respects to special chassis of Roadster.

The Motor Road Test No. 21/54 (Continental)

Make: Daimler   **Type:** Conquest Roadster

Makers: The Daimler Co., Limited, Coventry

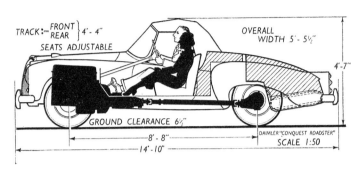

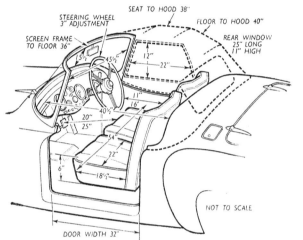

Test Data

CONDITIONS: Weather: Fine, warm, moderate cross wind. Surface: Smooth dry concrete (Ostend-Ghent motor road). Fuel: British and Belgian premium grades. Tests made with hood and side screens erected.

INSTRUMENTS
Speedometer at 30 m.p.h.	2% fast
Speedometer at 60 m.p.h.	2% fast
Speedometer at 90 m.p.h.	2% fast
Distance recorder	5% fast

MAXIMUM SPEEDS
Flying Quarter Mile
Mean of four opposite runs	100.7 m.p.h.
Best time equals	101.7 m.p.h.

Speed in gears
Max. speed in 3rd gear	72 m.p.h.
Max. speed in 2nd gear	48 m.p.h.

FUEL CONSUMPTION
34.5 m.p.g. at constant 30 m.p.h.
32.5 m.p.g. at constant 40 m.p.h.
28.0 m.p.g. at constant 50 m.p.h.
24.0 m.p.g. at constant 60 m.p.h.
22.0 m.p.g. at constant 70 m.p.h.
20.5 m.p.g. at constant 80 m.p.h.
17.5 m.p.g. at constant 90 m.p.h.
Overall consumption for 833 miles, 39 gallons, = 21.4 m.p.g.
Fuel tank capacity 15 gallons.

ACCELERATION TIMES Through gears
0-30 m.p.h.	4.9 sec.
0-40 m.p.h.	7.1 sec.
0-50 m.p.h.	10.6 sec.
0-60 m.p.h.	14.5 sec.
0-70 m.p.h.	20.0 sec
0-80 m.p.h.	28.0 sec.
0-90 m.p.h.	39.4 sec.
Standing Quarter Mile	20.3 sec.

ACCELERATION TIMES on Two Upper Ratios
	Top	3rd
10-30 m.p.h.	9.1 sec.	5.7 sec.
20-40 m.p.h.	9.3 sec.	6.0 sec.
30-50 m.p.h.	9.2 sec.	6.3 sec.
40-60 m.p.h.	10.4 sec.	7.4 sec.
50-70 m.p.h.	11.6 sec.	—
60-80 m.p.h.	13.5 sec.	—
70-90 m.p.h.	19.4 sec.	—

WEIGHT
Unladen kerb weight	25½ cwt.
Front/rear weight distribution	53/47
Weight laden as tested	29 cwt.

HILL CLIMBING (At steady speeds)
Max. top gear speed on 1 in 20	91 m.p.h.
Max. top gear speed on 1 in 15	85 m.p.h.
Max. top gear speed on 1 in 10	64 m.p.h.
Max. gradient on top gear	1 in 8.1 (Tapley 275 lb./ton)
Max. gradient on 3rd gear	1 in 5.6 (Tapley 395 lb./ton)
Max. gradient on 2nd gear	1 in 4.0 (Tapley 540 lb./ton)

BRAKES at 30 m.p.h.
0.87 g retardation (= 34½ ft. stopping distance) with 115 lb. pedal pressure.
0.85 g retardation (= 35½ ft. stopping distance) with 100 lb. pedal pressure.
0.70 g retardation (= 43 ft. stopping distance) with 75 lb. pedal pressure.
0.49 g retardation (= 61½ ft. stopping distance) with 50 lb. pedal pressure.
0.17 g retardation (=177 ft. stopping distance) with 25 lb. pedal pressure.

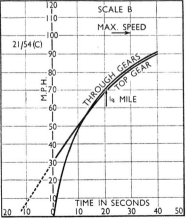

Drag at 10 m.p.h. .. 44 lb.
Drag at 60 m.p.h. .. 148 lb.

Specific Fuel Consumption when cruising at 80% of maximum speed (i.e. 80.6 m.p.h.) on level road, based on power delivered to rear wheels .. 0.69 pints/b.h.p./hr.

Maintenance

Sump: 10 pints, S.A.E. 30. **Gearbox:** 5½ pints, S.A.E. 30. **Rear Axle:** 2½ pints, S.A.E. 90. **Steering gear:** ⅓ pint, S.A.E. 90. **Radiator:** 17 pints (3 drain taps). **Chassis lubrication:** By oil gun every 1,000 miles to propeller shaft (3 points), grease gun every 3,000 miles to water pump (1 point) and every 6,000 miles to rear hubs (2 points); lubrication automatic to remaining 15 points. **Ignition timing:** 9 degrees B.T.D.C. **Spark plug gap:** 0.020 in. **Contact breaker gap:** 0.014—0.016 in. **Valve timing:** Inlet opens 13 degrees B.T.D.C. and closes 65 degrees A.B.D.C. Exhaust opens 55 degrees B.B.D.C. and closes 23 degrees A.T.D.C. **Tappet clearances:** (Hot) Inlet 0.013 in.; Exhaust 0.013 in. **Front wheel toe-in:** ⅛ in. **Camber angle:** 1½ degrees. **Castor angle:** Nil. **Tyre pressures:** Front 24 lb., rear 24 lb. **Brake fluid:** Girling Crimson. **Battery:** 12-volt, 51 amp./hr. **Lamp bulbs:** Headlamps, 45/35 watt (Lucas No. 360); **Long range auxiliary lamp,** 48 watt (Lucas No. 185); fog lamp, 48 watt (Lucas No. 323); side lamps, 6 watt (Lucas No. 207); **front direction indicator lamps and reversing lamps,** 18 watt (Lucas No. 221); **rear number plate lamp,** 4 watt (Lucas No. 222); **stop/tail/rear indicator lamps,** 18/6 watt (Lucas No. 361); **panel lights,** 6 watt (AC No. 1570839).

Ref. B/25/54

THE NEW DAIMLER DROPHEAD COUPE

100 MPH AND ALL THIS GREATER COMFORT

★ *Curve-backed seats for fast-cornering comfort.*

★ *Transverse seat behind driver, easily detachable.*

★ *New washable drophead-type hood with washable lining gives maximum headroom. The flexible rear window can be zipped down.*

★ *Snugly-fitting wind-up windows.*

★ *Heating equipment as standard.*

★ *Higher roof and wider doors give very easy entry.*

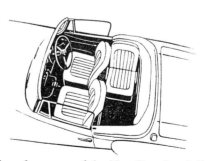

The vivid performance of the New Drophead Coupé is matched perfectly by sure, powerful braking, beautifully responsive steering and outstanding road holding. £1927.15.10 including purchase tax.

THE DAIMLER COMPANY LIMITED, RADFORD WORKS, COVENTRY

SUBLIME EASE OF HANDLING

...only one of the gifts of the
DAIMLER CONQUEST

The Fluid Transmission Conquest is a car you can park with virtually one foot! You simply set the hand-throttle to a fast tick-over—select your gear—then all you have to do is control the movement of the car with the foot brake only. This, combined with a remarkably small turning circle of 33 feet and a light steering action, makes handling really simple.

Speed with comfort — and good looks too. Ease of handling is not the only virtue of the Conquest. This fine car has pace—up to 60 in 20.4 seconds and on to an effortless top speed of 80 plus. *Laminated torsion bar suspension* gives absolutely faultless road-

holding. *Automatic chassis lubrication* provides continuous efficiency without thought or worry.

More rear-seat leg space. The Conquest is a fine-looking car with typical Daimler dignity. It is also roomy and comfortable, the new model having 4 inches more leg space in the rear seat. Price £1511. 5. 10 inclusive.

OTHER CONQUEST MODELS
The 'Conquest Century'......£1661. 9. 2. incl.
The Coupé........£1736. 10. 10. incl.
The Roadster......£1672. 15. 10. incl.

'Out of pedigree comes pace'

The 100 bhp Conquest Coupé
Power-operated drophead adjustable to three positions—closed, 'deville' and fully open.

THE DAIMLER COMPANY LIMITED · RADFORD WORKS · COVENTRY

5240

The versatility of the
DAIMLER CONQUEST COUPÉ

ONE CAR OR THREE? Take a good look at the Daimler Conquest Coupé. Here is a car which packs into one fine, elegant-looking body the attributes of three different kinds of car. With the power-operated hood folded away you have a fast open tourer that just laps up the miles. In seconds, when required, the hood comes up to the elegant 'de ville' position; and a further simple adjustment gives you a snug closed car with the warmth and comfort of a saloon. The hood is brought into action by a button under the dash. **Good manners at 90 m.p.h.** And what a thrill to drive. The special 100 bhp engine gives startlingly vivid acceleration and effortless cruising at 80 m.p.h. Braking is amazingly good, eliminating both 'fade' and skidding. As for road holding—just throw the Coupé into a fast bend, put your

At a touch of the button under the dash the power-operated hood comes from the open to the 'de ville' position.

foot down and see how superbly she takes you round. **Preselector fluid transmission.** There are many other points of the Coupé you will enjoy—preselector fluid transmission, automatic chassis lubrication, and the extremely high standard of comfort to which such features as a telescopic steering column and a built-in heater unit contribute so much. Altogether a quite exceptional kind of motoring for £1736. 10. 10 including purchase tax.

With the minimum handling the versatile hood gives the Conquest Coupé the warmth and comfort of a saloon.

B16

BY APPOINTMENT
Motor Car Manufacturers
to the late King George VI

THE DAIMLER COMPANY LIMITED, RADFORD WORKS, COVENTRY

Originally built for the personal use of Her Majesty Queen Elizabeth II.

284 1954 Daimler Century Mark II Saloon on Special Conquest Chassis

"Dauphin" coachwork by Hooper & Co. (Coachbuilders) Ltd.
Reg. No. ECG 342B
Chassis No. DJ256-90950
Engine No. 76207
Hooper Body No. 10014

Engine: Six cylinder in line, water-cooled monobloc, overhead valves, bore 76·2mm, stroke 88.9mm, capacity 2433cc. Four speed epicyclic gearbox with pre-selector change; Daimler fluid transmission coupling; hypoid bevel rear axle. Wheelbase 8ft. 8in. Tyres 6.70 × 15in.

ALPINE CONQUEST

Daimler and the Jungfrau, Grindelwald

CAPTIVATION OF A MOTORIST IN THE SWISS ALPS

LET me be frank. The name Daimler had, for many years, meant to me some excellent things: good engineering, good *engineers*, fluid flywheels and a fluted radiator. Also the dignity conferred on the company by her late Majesty Queen Mary's constant use of the make. A brief experience of the earlier 2½-litre suggested that there was something extra to dignity and tradition, and the performance of Conquests in sporting events of recent years emphasized the point. But in spite of all that, this 1,471-mile tour in the Conquest Century saloon was a revelation. The Conquest Century is one of those cars that is right, absolutely right. Let me amplify the statement.

I took over the car in a busy street and had to drive it two hundred yards to an awkward car park. It was so long since I had used the Daimler transmission that I had to sit and think of the motions. London traffic was eyeing me malevolently, and if there had been a policeman there I am sure that he would have told me to move on. Gingerly, I moved the finger-light lever in the quadrant to 1, gave the gear change pedal the customary push down and release, removed the hand brake and glided silently off. "Glided silently" is no cliché, as will become apparent. As I turned into the car park I could feel the pleasurable anticipation rising—I was going to like this car. All these miles later, I feel that more strongly than ever.

What is the specification for this degree of "rightness"? First, the engine: Daimlers are powered by an overhead-valve six giving 100 b.h.p. at 4,400 r.p.m. and a maximum torque of 130 lb ft at 2,500 r.p.m. It is a long-stroke unit, the vertical sweep being 88.9 mm, against which the bore is 76.2 mm; the length of the stroke by comparison with the bore is better judged by the inch figure: bore 3in, stroke 3½in. Capacity is 2,433 c.c. and compression ratio 7.75 to 1, a high ratio conferred by the light alloy head. Fuel is fed through two S.U. carburettors and the crankshaft gets its impulses on a 1-5-3-6-2-4 firing order. Added to all this is the Daimler know-how of this type of engine, and the first illustration of it is the fact that you cannot tell when the engine has responded to the starter; it's too quiet.

All right, you may argue—if some of those hundred brake horse-powers are sacrificed to silencing, so be it. But the car must feel it with a weight of 3,024 lb. The answer to

By MICHAEL BROWN

that is that it does not seem to. The Century gets under way with a will, the power unit responding to the throttle all the way up to 4,500 r.p.m. with what I feel to be a well-planned arc of foot movement. It is, moreover, the silkiest engine that I can recall, although it is fair to admit that I have not yet driven the latest from Conduit Street. On the other hand, I do not see how the virtual perfection of the Daimler engine in this particular respect can be surpassed. I must go up to Coventry and investigate the Daimler pursuit of silence and silkiness; there must be a story there.

However, we are concerned in this article with performance rather than design. Yet a little more is needed about design if the performance is to be fully conveyed. The Conquest has the famous fluid flywheel transmission with the epicyclic gear box, and this plays no small part in the delight of Daimler driving. It is some time since its operation was detailed in these columns: there is a two-finger type of lever working in a quadrant on the right of the steering column, the lever being positioned so that the wheel rim need not be released by the right hand. The quadrant has four positions above neutral (N): 1, 2, 3, T; and one below: R, with a stop to obviate inadvertent engagement, for this is reverse.

The actual change is effected by the depression and release of a pedal exactly like a clutch pedal. However, the release should not be gentle, but just as decisive as the depression. It is, in fact, a foot gear change, and the only judgment required is that governing engine speed.

Driver sequence, therefore, is this for a move off from rest: move quadrant lever to 1, actuate gear pedal. The car is now ready to move off but is held by the hand brake. Release the brake and away it goes, almost imperceptibly, just creeping forward without the slightest fear of a stall, or a run-back when the hand brake is released: admirable.

Summit, Furka Pass, Switzerland

Left : Hotel Jungfrau - Victoria, Interlaken

Right : Euclidean pattern, Inter- laken

ALPINE CONQUEST . . .

speedometer which I judged to be quite accurate. For long stretches at 75 m.p.h. it was equally unstressed, and we saw the needle on much higher figures at times.

Having no great interest in maximum speed, I did not pursue the ultimate; my motoring interests lie in how a car does its intended job of carrying its passengers and luggage over the distances.

The Conquest Century does the job very well. At the front, the wheels are suspended by laminated torsion bars with wishbones and telescopic dampers; rear suspension is by half-elliptics. These laminated bars seem to give rather more softness and amplitude than the solid bar, but any tendency for the fact to be apparent on corners is prevented by an anti-roll bar at the front. The result is a happy one, though a driver feels slightly guilty as he hauls this luxury saloon round with a quick turn of the steering wheel and feels the car slide gently under the deliberately too-high speed. Nothing untowards happens, the car responding to correction in an orthodox way, leaving behind the temptation to do it again.

On mountain hairpins the admirable lock is appreciated. The Furka is a "tight" pass on the corners, but on no

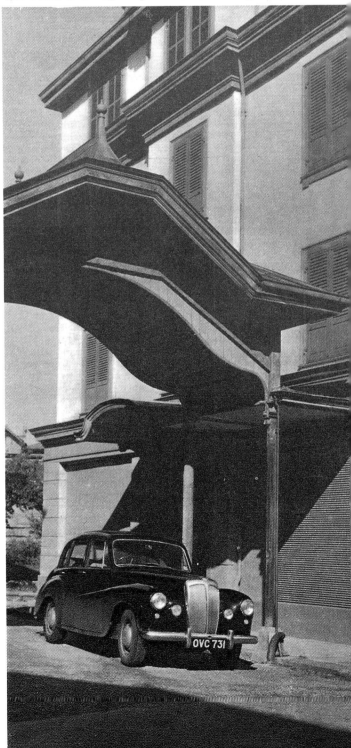

You may now preselect the next gear up. Move the lever to 2, but make the actual change at any time subsequently, for selection does not demand immediate change. And so you continue to play with this delightful transmission; and just to make things additionally easy, the Conquest has a hand throttle, enabling you to set a certain engine speed for lengthy manœuvring in close quarters, leaving the right foot free for braking. When U.S. transmissions are being adulated, it is well to recall this long-established British transmission that is so remarkably clever while leaving the driver in absolute control of performance. If I were not still an overgrown schoolboy (and rather glad of the fact) I would fall for this system; in fact, I may well do so when my stirring days (with, for preference, a six-inch gear lever) are over.

On down the transmission line is the Hardy-Spicer shaft and a hypoid bevel final drive. These are the ratios that go with the transmission (overall): 4.56, 6.71, 10.05 and 17.47 to 1. Reverse is 23.7 to 1.

For the first few miles with this type of propulsion, the driver accustomed to the conventional box needs to think. If I were a Daimler salesman, therefore, I would be generous with my demonstration runs, allowing the prospective customer a couple of hundred miles to succumb to the ease of control. I found that the changes were subconscious after about this distance, and that, if I did think about them, I could even make them imperceptibly. There is nothing more flattering to the conceit. As to reversing, hotel and garage staff are most impressed. Here, they obviously say, is a man in complete control of his affairs. Just look! He creeps back, silently, smoothly, at less than a mile an hour. (The triumph is short-lived; the porter has spotted the radiator.)

Normal starting from rest does not call for first, this ratio being there for really steep slopes. In second the car surges forward and the change-up point seems to settle instinctively at about 20 m.p.h. Third continues up to a similarly instinctive 40, and then you are in a top that takes the car along at any speed over a wide cruising range. It is exceedingly happy when 65-70 m.p.h. are showing on a

ALPINE CONQUEST . . .

occasion was the Daimler forced unduly out from its side of the road. The only criticism I would make of the Daimler's cornering should, I suppose, be addressed to Fort Dunlop, for it was a most embarrassing squealer on dry roads. However, tyre pressures were a bit low. It is high time that the tyre manufacturers got down to the elimination of squeal at normal speeds.

The car revelled in the long climbs of the Swiss passes. Most cars should, but there are some whose gear ratios fall unhappily for the long, steady gradients. In second, the Conquest climbed easily and with a scarcely perceptible shift of the thermometer needle. Power loss with height was not evident, but the car was, in any case, lightly laden, and was touring, not a-rallying. Besides which, the driver likes to admire the scenery.

In the narrow Alpine towns there could be no easier mount. A Daimler will trickle when other engines have begun to gulp; it will turn a prop-shaft steadily when other cars want a slipped clutch, and for anyone to whom engagement of first gear in motion has terrors, a fluid flywheel is the answer. Change into first on the Daimler is just the same as changing into any other lower ratio. All that is needed is the appropriate speed-up of the engine.

Much of the pleasure of this close-quarter technique comes from the driving position. The driver's half of the optional bench seat can be adjusted to fit snugly round his shoulders at just about the right distance from the pedals. The telescopic steering wheel can then be brought into the family harmony, for its angle is right and its feel admirable. There is no suggestion in this position of control by a liveried James awaiting instructions (though James would enjoy driving the Conquest) but of a keen motorist getting down to the business of fast, silent, comfortable travel from here to there.

The riding comfort has the quality that derives from a high sprung to unsprung weight ratio. The Conquest retains the traditional frame of long side members and a cruciform centre, and the bodywork is also traditional, woodwork in the shape of honey-coloured oak surrounding the driver, in company with fine leather and thick carpets. This is heavy construction, and the owner who likes the feeling of luxury must be prepared for the fact.

But weight is certainly not all drawback; minor indentations in road surfaces are ironed out completely, and major ones are felt only if the wave that they form in the road is of the right frequency to excite a sympathetic rise and fall of the chassis. When that happens one must slow down, and it is, perhaps, more likely with a car having a high ratio between sprung and unsprung masses than with the opposite, owing to pendulum effect. There were certain road wave frequencies on the French and Swiss roads which caught the Conquest, but not many.

In the Wet

The rain—and it rained during most of the trip—seemed to have very little effect on performance. It was a little easier to make the car slide in the wet, although the brakes —hydromechanical—seemed to take hold just as well and without locking the wheels; they really worked on the Conquest, biting so hard at times that grab was suspected. The wipers wiped the very deep screen effectively and the car was watertight. With four ventilating flaps it was possible to ventilate adequately without the heating system, though the driver having got wet outside the car one day, the heater was given a trial for laundry purposes and effectively produced a Turkish bath temperature in an ambient temperature around the seventies.

Most of the fitments are calculated to please. As one who likes driving for its own sake, I appreciated the array of instruments—a full one including a rev counter, though the oil pressure indicator is only a warning lamp. Ash trays are big, sensible, and mounted on the doors; there are arm rests all round, a lockable locker on the left and an open miniature on the driver's side. Lighting is effective, responding to a foot dip-switch, and a rheostat controls the

Frontier, Les Verrières-de-Joux

panel brightness. The interior light is central in a cloth roof lining and is independently switched from the door pillars.

Under the bonnet the dipstick is admirable and the long, well-finished engine a joy to behold. No joy, however, comes from my contemplation of a lockable filler cap, for I hate the fussy things. The luggage locker is big, though one must get under the upward-opening lid for good stowage.

I like the appearance except for one absurd disappointment, and that is because nothing of the fine grille is visible from the driving seat. I do not know where Daimlers will go next in terms of appearance, but they certainly need not lose their characteristic grille, even if they eventually produce an orifice like that of the Le Mans M.G. As a matter of fact, London County Council ambulances for years have demonstrated a smart modern adaptation of the flutes on their straight eight vehicles.

Petrol consumption? About 22 m.p.g. over the 1,471-mile journey. Oil consumption was about six pints. Remember also that in the buying price of £1,661 you are provided with automatic chassis lubrication worked on thermostatic principles. Under "Every Thousand Miles" in the instruction book is a solitary entry: "Lubricate the propeller-shaft." There are three nipples involved, and you start real maintenance work only after each 3,000 miles have passed.

What a nice car it is, to be sure. Just right for the sporting owner-driver, who would enjoy looking after it like a mountaineer does his ice-axe. The Alpine Conquest of the title involves no Matterhorns, but it does suggest what happened to a driver whose ideas of Daimlers were running in too-traditional grooves.

The new Daimler 2½ litre 'Century' Mk. II saloon

Get there swifter...
safer...fresher...
Drive DAIMLER

The NEW 1956 Daimler Range:

DAIMLER "CONQUEST" 2½ LITRE

'Conquest Mk. II' Saloon	.. ..	£1,735. 7. 0
'Century Mk. II' Saloon	.. ..	£1,897. 7. 0
The New Drophead Coupé	..	£2,041. 7. 0

DAIMLER 3½ LITRE and 4½ LITRE MODELS

3½ litre 'One-O-Four' Saloon	..	£2,828. 17. 0
3½ litre 'One-O-Four' Lady's Model	..	*£3,076. 7. 0
4½ litre 4-light Saloon	..	£3,440. 17. 0
4½ litre DK.400 Limousine	.. ..	£4,190. 17. 0

(All prices include purchase tax)

*This new reduced price enables the special Lady's items to be purchased as optional extras item by item to choice.

The Daimler Company Limited, Radford Works, Coventry

ALL-ROUND VISIBILITY

D277

...only one of the gifts of the
DAIMLER CONQUEST

Sit behind the wheel of the Daimler Conquest and you feel complete master of the situation. The comfortably high driving position, while giving even a tall man plenty of head room, takes maximum advantage of the curved windscreen, slender pillars, extensive side and rear windows and well placed driving mirror. The twin windscreen wipers sweep an exceptionally wide area and provide a big overlap in the middle, effectively cutting out wet-weather blind spots.

But as well as good visibility, the Conquest gives you magnificent performance and road holding, and offers such notable features as preselector fluid transmission and automatic chassis lubrication.

Comfort and dignity with dash. The Conquest is a fine-looking car, combining dignity and comfort with tremendous dash. Both front and rear compartments are spacious, with widely opening doors for easy access. Price £1511. 5. 10 including purchase tax.

OTHER CONQUEST MODELS

The 'Conquest Century' ...... £1661. 9. 2. incl.
The Coupé ..... £1736. 10. 10. incl.
The Roadster ... £1672. 15. 10. incl.

'Out of pedigree comes pace'

The 100 bhp Century: *twin carburettors, bigger brakes, telescopic steering column, rev. counter. From 0-60 in 16.3 seconds and over 90 in top.*

THE DAIMLER COMPANY LIMITED · RADFORD WORKS · COVENTRY

By Appointment To Her Majesty the Queen, Motor Car Manufacturers The Daimler Co. Ltd.

Improved Daimler Conquest and Century Saloons

The Daimler Company Ltd. introduce new Conquest and Century Saloon models

THE CONQUEST Mk 11

75 b.h.p. Saloon. Price: £1156 plus P.T. £579-7-0

THE CENTURY Mk 11

100 b.h.p. Saloon. Price: £1264 plus P.T. £633-7-0

Improvements include—completely new and highly efficient heater, de-mister and ventilation unit; lighting system with spread beam fog lamp and penetrating beam lamp; greatly improved frontal appearance. The luxurious interior of the Century model is enhanced with handsome polished *burr* walnut throughout for facia and all woodwork fittings: the Conquest model has all woodwork in polished walnut.

For a blend of performance, comfort and craftsmanship, these cars are absolutely unsurpassed in their field. Their acceleration, their ease of handling. their superb road holding, have made them world-famous.

D295

The Daimler Company Limited, Radford Works, Coventry

—The Daimler Century Saloon

(with Automatic Transmission)

A Fast 2½-litre Saloon in which Tradition is Pleasantly Blended with Modern Amenities

AS the founders of the Motor Industry, the Daimler company have a long and distinguished tradition, which is strongly evident in the Century saloon. Although a completely post-war design, it carries the unmistakeable stamp of a car in which a strong belief in what is best has nowhere been submerged by what is most expedient (or cheap) to produce.

One member of the staff who tried the Century described it succinctly as vintage motoring with modern amenities—and if the word vintage is interpreted in its best sense that is no inapt description. Certainly the Century is a car which appeals strongly to the connoisseur on the grounds of sound engineering, refined behaviour and high quality of detail and finish; but that is not all. The Century offers, in addition, an honest 90 m.p.h. maximum speed and acceleration which is much brisker than the unobtrusive manner of its production might suggest. A stop watch time of 12.8 seconds to reach 50 m.p.h. from rest places it easily in the faster category of touring cars.

The model tested was equipped with Borg-Warner fully-automatic transmission which is now offered (at an extra cost of £185 inclusive of tax) as an alternative to the fluid flywheel and pre-selector gearbox which have been exclusive Daimler features for 25 years. The choice seems a logical one because the two systems have a certain amount in common, but the Borg-Warner system has the additional refinement of a torque converter and fully automatic operation.

Fluid Transmission

Thus, apart from its general merits—which are notable—the Borg-Warner system will prove particularly attractive to previous Daimler owners who have strong leanings towards a fluid flywheel or its equivalent and would not, in many cases, consider a car without one. To such, the Borg-Warner system represents a natural step forward and one with which they will immediately feel at home. It is a system, moreover, which suits the Century particularly well in its refined and unobtrusive behaviour.

To most readers of *The Motor* the Borg-Warner transmission is already familiar. In brief, it consists of a torque converter working in conjunction with automatically operated epicyclic gearing. The converter serves to take care of starts from rest (there is no clutch pedal, of course) and also augments the effect of the two lower gears by a torque multiplication which virtually gives a variable ratio for low and intermediate gears. In top gear, a special clutch by-passes the converter to give a direct drive in the interests of fuel economy.

Engagement of the appropriate gear for any given conditions takes place quite automatically when the small control lever is placed in "Drive," and varies according to the speed and load. Thus, a very leisurely start from rest with minimum throttle opening will result in intermediate gear being engaged at approximately 10 m.p.h. and top at approximately 20 m.p.h., but if the throttle is fully opened, these changing speeds are delayed in the case of the Daimler to approximately 25 m.p.h. and 48 m.p.h. In addition, the throttle is provided with a kick-down action by which it can be held beyond the normal fully-open position for utmost acceleration or power, this either delaying the change to the maximum speed predetermined by the manufacturers for the gear concerned or causing the appropriate lower gear to be engaged if the car is travelling appreciably below that speed. The actual maxima for the Century are 35 m.p.h. in bottom gear and 60 m.p.h. in intermediate.

In practice, this transmission works extremely well, being notably smooth, quiet and restful in operation. It can, in fact, be criticized on only two counts, neither of them serious. One is the slight bound forward which occurs as a result of engine inertia when a higher gear is engaged; this is satisfying rather than otherwise when acceleration is being continued, but slightly irritating when the higher gear goes home as one eases the throttle to tuck into a gap in traffic.

The other minor disadvantage is that, by the very nature of things, engine tick-over speeds must be strictly limited if the car is not to creep in gear. With a warm engine, no difficulties arise but, after

The Daimler Century

LARGE swivelling quarter windows make the Century virtually a six-light saloon. The bulged boot lid has a very practical virtue in permitting really bulky luggage to be carried.

initial start in cold weather, a rather tricky balance has to be struck between an over-fast tick-over and over-richness which would cause stalling. The fact that the Century engine is not so quick as some to warm up rather emphasizes this minor dilemma which can, however, be overcome by allowing the engine to idle with the gear in neutral for a short time before starting off.

Starting itself is particularly sure and the modern type of ignition-cum-starter switch a convenience. At all times, the engine is particularly unobtrusive and has that pleasant feeling of an inherently well-balanced unit rather than one which gains its effect of sweetness from flexible mountings. There is a subtle difference between the two.

So far as actual performance is concerned the figures may largely be left to tell their own story showing, as they do, the Century to be a very lively but economical example of a 2½-litre saloon. In particular, the performance at the top end of the range is good.

Judged by touring car standards—and it is as a luxurious medium-powered family or professional car rather than as a sports car that the Century must be regarded—the suspension and handling qualities are good. The suspension is by means of laminated torsion bars at the front and a pleasantly-firm but very comfortable ride is provided, that bugbear of so many modern cars, road-noise, being almost entirely absent.

On corners, the Century normally displays a degree of understeer, but this is most pronounced at low speeds and can be changed to the opposite characteristic by hard acceleration. There is no pitching and comparatively little roll, whilst the car follows a straight course with little attention on the part of the driver.

On the model tried, however, a slight front-end dither could be detected through the wheel at high speeds and, although this never reached serious proportions, it did detract somewhat from the pleasure of fast driving. The steering itself is moderately geared and slightly on the heavy side when manœuvring in confined spaces, but an outstandingly good point is the excellent lock provided for a car of this size. The brakes, too, are good and more than normally light in operation. Of the pistol-grip type, the handbrake is reasonably accessible and well capable of holding the car on a severe gradient.

Interior planning of the driving compartment is suggestive of designers who are themselves keen drivers and is perhaps one of the reasons why this car is so easy to drive in traffic. The large thin-rimmed spring wheel is at a comfortable angle and possesses that now-rare refinement of an extending column, whilst the pedals move through natural arcs and are well spaced. The facia board houses a comprehensive array of good quality instruments, sensibly but tastefully laid out on a beautifully-finished walnut veneer centre panel flanked by cubby holes. Logical circular dials are used, with the equally logical choice of white figures and hands against a black background, and variable illumination is provided.

Minor Controls

Refinements include a large-dial rev. counter, a hand-throttle, a reserve petrol control (which is deliberately obtrusive when in the reserve position) and a screen washer. The lighting switch, incidentally, also controls the fog lamps when turned to beyond the "head" position, but a separate switch is provided so that one or both may be used, this controlling the offside auxiliary lamp which is of the pencil-beam type capable of being set to pick out either kerb or cats-eyes according to the driver's own particular technique in fog.

The deep screen and large window area provide a good all-round view, although the somewhat high bonnet hides the near-side wing for a driver of normal stature.

LEATHER and polished woodwork give the car an air of sober quality. The photograph above shows how the control for the Borg-Warner automatic transmission fits naturally into the place normally occupied by the pre-selector quadrant. Instruments are clear and well calibrated.

Saloon

A FLAT floor to the boot has straps built-in to provide anchorage for single items of luggage; the boot lid is counterbalanced, but there is no interior illumination.

A praiseworthy minor point is that the rear-view mirror is efficient without forming an obstruction to forward vision, whilst another good mark is earned by the excellent side vision through the rear quarters. The latter are arranged to open for ventilation as well as the normal ventilating panels on the front doors; these latter, however, have only one ideal open position; at small openings they are apt to cause a whistle and at wide openings a wind-roar, either of which disturbs the silence of an otherwise outstandingly quiet car.

A fresh-air type of heater and demister is provided as standard and not only supplies an adequate degree of heat, but also has the advantage of directing it on the occupants' feet.

Comfortable seating is a Daimler tradition and the Century is no exception. The separately adjustable front seats have that firm but well-shaped upholstery which permits long occupation without fatigue and the high slightly curved squabs give plenty of lateral support without cramping. Much the same applies to the rear, where the car is notable for the unusually generous knee-room. The Century is, however, primarily a four-seater although it will, of course, take five on occasion. Nicely placed arm-rests are provided on all the doors and ease of entry is an outstanding feature, but lack of courtesy switches on the doors is an unexpected omission.

In the matter of luggage, the boot comes as a surprise as, owing to the curvature of the top-hinged counterbalanced lid, it gives much more room than a casual glance suggests. The fact that a sizeable cabin trunk was accommodated at one stage gives a good idea of its capacity. The luggage floor (above the spare wheel) is perfectly flat and a typical refinement is the provision of straps, with hooked ends engaging in flush staples so that a single object can be positively located. Rather surprisingly, no boot illumination is provided.

Walnut and Leather

As will already have been gathered, the finish and furnishing of this Daimler are in the best traditions. Not only is the facia board of polished walnut, but the same wood is provided for the door cappings whilst the entire upholstery trim is carried out in high-grade leather which gives a sober suggestion of luxury as well as being very hard-wearing. There are, moreover, no crude corners such as one finds on many popular cars, whilst detail refinements include flush-fitting vizors (slightly too deep for tall occupants, however) and spring-up arm slings in the rear. In accordance with Daimler practice, it is the nearside door which locks with a key and although some prefer this arrangement, the more conventional plan of the driver's door locking is generally to be preferred. Typically Daimler is a really comprehensive set of high-grade tools and another most important mechanical feature is an automatic chassis lubrication system.

In short, the Century is a car which will appeal strongly to the man who likes good things for what they are as well as for their functional merit. Providing a degree of luxury which is less common now than it was, coupled with quiet and above all restful motoring, the Century nevertheless boasts of a performance well in keeping with other cars of its class.

Specification

Engine

Cylinders	6
Bore	76.2 mm.
Stroke	88.9 mm.
Cubic capacity	2,433 c.c.
Piston area	42.4 sq. in.
Valves	Overhead (push-rod)
Compression ratio	7.75/1
Carburetters	Two S.U. (horizontal)
Fuel pump	AC mechanical
Ignition timing control	Centrifugal and vacuum
Oil filter	Tecalemit full-flow
Max. power (gross)	100 b.h.p.
at	4,400 r.p.m.
Piston speed at max. b.h.p.	2,570 ft./min.

Transmission

Borg-Warner automatic transmission (incorporating torque converter).

Top gear	4.09 (direct drive)
Intermediate	5.869
	(11.74 with max. torque multiplication)
Low	9.44
	(18.88 with max. torque multiplication)
Reverse	8.217
	(16.43 with max. torque multiplication)
Propeller shaft	Open, divided Hardy Spicer
Final drive	Hypoid bevel
Top gear m.p.h. at 1,000 r.p.m.	19.4
Top gear m.p.h. at 1,000 ft./min. piston speed	25.0

Chassis

Brakes	Girling hydro-mechanical (2LS on front)
Brake drum internal diameter	11 in.
Friction lining area	184 sq. in.
Suspension:	
Front	Independent (laminated torsion bars)
Rear	Semi-elliptic
Shock absorbers	Girling telescopic
Steering gear	High-efficiency Bishop cam
Tyres	Dunlop 6.70—15 (tubeless)

Coachwork and Equipment

Starting handle	Yes
Battery mounting	Under rear seat (l.h. side)
Jack	Bevelift, screw type
Jacking points	Two front, two rear on chassis frame

Standard tool kit: Three double-ended spanners, plug box spanner and tommy bar, hub cap spanner, adjustable spanner, pair pliers, screwdriver, distributor screwdriver and feeler gauge, hub cap remover, oil gun, grease gun, wheelbrace, tool roll and tool bag for jack.

Exterior lights: Two headlamps, two fog lamps, two side lamps, two tail/stop lamps, rear number plate lamp and reversing light.

Number of electrical fuses	Two
Direction indicators	Semaphore arm type
Windscreen wipers	Electric, self-parking
Windscreen washers	Electric
Sun vizors	Two

Instruments: Speedometer (with trip), rev. counter fuel gauge, ammeter, thermometer, clock.

Warning lights: Oil, ignition, trafficators, headlamp main beam.	
Locks:	
With ignition key	Front passenger's door, boot and petrol filler cap
With other keys	None
Glove lockers: Two (without lids); one for front passenger (with sub-division for instruction book) and one for driver.	
Pockets	Four (one in each door)
Parcel shelves	One (behind rear squab)
Ashtrays	Four(one in each front door and one in back of each front squab)
Cigar lighters	None
Interior lights	One (in roof)
Interior heater	Smith's FHF 3503, 3½ k/w. heater and demister (fresh-air type)
Extras available	Radio
Upholstery material	Leather
Floor covering	Felt-backed pile carpets
Number of exterior colours standardized: Three duo-tone finishes and five single colours.	
Alternative body styles	Drop-head coupé

Maintenance

Sump	10 pints, S.A.E. 10/30 multi-viscosity
Gearbox:	15 pints, Esso Automatic Transmission Fluid 55, Mobilfluid 200, Shell Donax T6 or Castrol T.Q.
Rear axle	2½ pints, S.A.E. 90
Steering gear lubricant	S.A.E. 90
Cooling system capacity	18 pints (two drain taps and one plug)
Chassis lubrication: By automatic thermal system to front suspension and steering; by grease gun up to water pump and propeller shaft universals every 1,000 miles.	
Ignition timing	9° b.t.d.c. static
Contact-breaker gap	0.014-0.016 in.
Sparking plug type	Lodge CLNH
Sparking plug gap	0.025 in.

Valve timing: Inlet opens 13° b.t.d.c. and closes 65° a.b.d.c.; exhaust opens 55° b.b.d.c. and closes 23° a.t.d.c.

Tappet clearances (hot):	
Inlet	0.013 in.
Exhaust	0.013 in.
Front wheel toe-in	⅛ in.
Camber angle	1¼°
Castor angle	0°
Steering swivel pin inclination	8°
Tyre pressures:	
Front	24 lb.
Rear	26 lb.
Brake fluid	Girling Crimson
Battery type and capacity	Lucas G.T.W. 9A, 51 amp./hr.
Miscellaneous	Top up automatic chassis lubrication reservoir monthly

The Motor Road Test No. 18/57

Make: Daimler   **Type: Century Saloon**

Makers: The Daimler Co., Ltd., Coventry.

Test Data

CONDITIONS: *Weather: Cold, dry, light wind. (Temperature 38°—46° F., Barometer 30.1 in. Hg.) Surface: Smooth dry tar macadam. Fuel: Premium grade pump petrol, approx. 95 Research Method Octane Rating.*

INSTRUMENTS

Speedometer at 30 m.p.h.	.. ..	3% slow
Speedometer at 60 m.p.h.	.. ..	accurate
Speedometer at 80 m.p.h.	.. ..	2% fast
Distance recorder	.. ..	accurate

WEIGHT

Kerb weight, (unladen, but with oil, coolant and fuel for approx. 50 miles)   29 cwt.
Front/rear distribution of kerb weight   52/48
Weight laden as tested .. .. .. 32½ cwt.

MAXIMUM SPEEDS
Flying Quarter Mile

Mean of two flying laps of banked circuit .. .. 90.4 m.p.h.
Best one-way timed ¼-mile on straight 92.8 m.p.h.

"Maximile" Speed. (Timed quarter mile after one mile accelerating from rest)
Mean .. .. 88.2 m.p.h.
Best one-way time equals .. 90.0 m.p.h.

Speed in Gears
Max. speed in intermediate gear .. 60 m.p.h.
Max. speed in low gear .. .. .. 35 m.p.h.

FUEL CONSUMPTION

35.0 m.p.g. at constant 30 m.p.h. on level.
31.5 m.p.g. at constant 40 m.p.h. on level.
29.0 m.p.g. at constant 50 m.p.h. on level.
25.5 m.p.g. at constant 60 m.p.h. on level.
21.5 m.p.g. at constant 70 m.p.h. on level.
18.5 m.p.g. at constant 80 m.p.h. on level.

Overall Fuel Consumption for 826 miles, 35.2 gallons, equals 23.5 m.p.g. (12.0 litres/100 km.).

Touring Fuel Consumption (m.p.g. at steady speed midway between 30 m.p.h. and maximum, less 5% allowance for acceleration). 24.1 m.p.g.

Fuel Tank Capacity (maker's figure) 15 gallons (Incl. 1½ gall. reserve).

STEERING

Turning circle between kerbs:
Left.. .. .. 34 ft.
Right .. .. 31 ft.
Turns of steering wheel from lock to lock 3¼

BRAKES from 30 m.p.h.

0.92g retardation (equivalent to 33 ft. stopping distance) with 90 lb. pedal pressure
0.89g retardation (equivalent to 34 ft. stopping distance) with 75 lb. pedal pressure
0.66g retardation (equivalent to 60 ft. stopping distance) with 50 lb. pedal pressure
0.30g retardation (equivalent to 100 ft. stopping distance) with 25 lb. pedal pressure

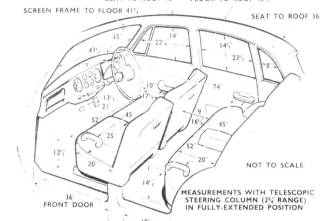

TRACK: FRONT 4·4 / REAR 4·4
OVERALL WIDTH 5·6
5·4½
21¼   20¼
12¼   11¼
GROUND CLEARANCE 6"
SCALE 1:50 →   8'·8½"   DAIMLER CENTURY
14'·9½"

SEAT TO ROOF 42"   FLOOR TO ROOF 45½"
SCREEN FRAME TO FLOOR 41¼"   SEAT TO ROOF 36"
15"   14"   22¼"   14½"
43½"   23¼"   8"
10"   74"
13½"   21"
52"   45"   9"
25"   16½"   45"
12½"   52"
20"   20"   NOT TO SCALE
14½"
36" FRONT DOOR
19" REAR DOOR
SEATS ADJUSTABLE
MEASUREMENTS WITH TELESCOPIC STEERING COLUMN (2¼" RANGE) IN FULLY-EXTENDED POSITION

ACCELERATION TIMES from standstill
(Kick-down condition).

0-30 m.p.h.	.. .. ..	6.4 sec.
0-40 m.p.h.	.. .. ..	9.1 sec.
0-50 m.p.h.	.. .. ..	12.8 sec.
0-60 m.p.h.	.. .. ..	17.7 sec.
0-70 m.p.h.	.. .. ..	25.8 sec.
0-80 m.p.h.	.. .. ..	39.1 sec.
Standing quarter mile	.. ..	21.8 sec.

ACCELERATION TIMES in Drive Range

			Top-Gear condition	Kick-down
0-20 m.p.h.	.. ..	—	4.1 sec.
10-30 m.p.h.	.. ..	—	4.5 sec.
20-40 m.p.h.	.. ..	—	5.1 sec.
30-50 m.p.h.	.. ..	10.6 sec.	6.4 sec.
40-60 m.p.h.	.. ..	12.1 sec.	8.5 sec.
50-70 m.p.h.	.. ..	15.0 sec.	13.0 sec.
60-80 m.p.h.	.. ..	21.4 sec.	21.4 sec.

HILL CLIMBING at sustained steady speeds

Max. gradient on top gear   1 in 10.6 (Tapley 210 lb. ton)
Max. gradient on intermediate gear
   1 in 6.7 (Tapley 330 lb. ton)

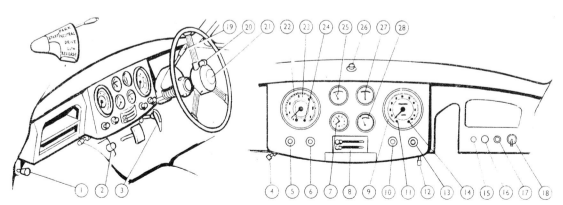

1, Bonnet catch release. 2, Headlamp dip switch. 3, Handbrake. 4, Clock adjuster. 5, Petrol reserve control. 6, Panel light switch. 7, Clock. 8, Heater and demister controls. 9, Speedometer with distance recorder and trip. 10, Mixture control. 11, Direction indicator warning light. 12, Trip re-setting knob. 13, Hand throttle. 14, Main beam indicator light. 15, Fog lamp switch. 16, Windscreen wipers control. 17, Ignition and starter switch. 18, Lights switch. 19, Transmission selector lever. 20, Direction indicator switch. 21, Horn button. 22, Oil pressure warning light. 23, Tachometer. 24, Dynamo charge warning light. 25, Fuel contents gauge. 26, Windscreen washers control. 27, Ammeter. 28, Coolant thermometer.

B8

DAIMLER CONQUEST AND CENTURY

1953-54 MODELS

First published in
MOTOR TRADER
August 25, 1954

Manufacturers. The Daimler Co., Ltd., Radford Works, Coventry.

Except for minor details the exterior of the Century is similar to the Conquest, shown here

INTRODUCED at the Earls Court Motor Show of 1953, the Daimler Conquest appeared as the evolution from the Consort model of earlier production. Bearing a likeness to the earlier saloon models, the Conquest has a re-designed engine and restyled body, following the general trend of unit body construction.

The Century saloon, Coupé and Roadster models are all variations of the Conquest design and in this service sheet the principal variations are listed and described.

Mechanical changes which have taken place, apart from engine developments to produce greater power-to-weight ratio, are evident in the adoption of torsion bar front suspension, and gearbox and final drive ratios have been altered to suit performance of now more nearly "square" engine characteristics.

For reference and identification the chassis serial number with the type symbol D.J. is found on the off side of the chassis frame forward of the scuttle. Engine number appears stamped on the petrol pump boss on the near side of the engine. The chassis and engine numbers are also marked on a plate fixed to the engine side of the bulkhead on the off side of the car.

Some special tools are required. Unified threads and hexagons are used throughout (Whitworth in aluminium).

ENGINE

Mounting

At front, feet rest on bonded rubber pads bolted to engine and chassis frame brackets.

At rear, gearbox has bracket bolted to central member of bonded rubber sandwich assembly, of which outer plates, separated by distance-pieces, are bolted to short cross-member which, in turn, is bolted below chassis frame cruciform members. Gearbox rests on conical rubber buffer on cross-member. Tighten all bolts fully. Torque stops should be set after engine mountings have been tightened, so that both are just touching lug on rear engine plate.

Removal

Engine and gearbox can be removed as unit after removal of radiator and front wing assembly. Detach bonnet top from hinges, remove two bolts holding radiator cradle to front cross-member. Remove top and bottom water hoses. Disconnect wiring and connections from valances, and lift off complete assembly of front wings and radiator.

In the coupé the general lines of the body resemble the Conquest

Strikingly modern lines with twin tail fins distinguish the Roadster

Disconnect all pipes, wires and controls from engine and gearbox, including speedo drive and front end of propeller shaft. Detach front mountings from engine and rear mounting from gearbox bracket, and remove upper torque reaction buffer. Take weight of engine on sling passed under manifold and water pump, and lift out over front cross-member.

When reassembling front wings and radiator, note that radiator cradle rests on square rubber blocks, with round rubber blocks below, spigoted into cross-member. Tighten self-locking nuts only enough to nip rubbers firmly.

Crankshaft

Four main bearings. Thin steel-backed, white metal-lined shells located by tabs. End float controlled by half thrust washers located in either side of front main bearing cap. Washers available in three thicknesses: .0920, .0945 and .0970. No hand fitting permissible. Crankshaft must be kept forward whilst removing damper otherwise thrust washers will fall into sump. Wedge a piece of wood through inspection cover in bell housing which will push flywheel forward.

Main bearings cannot be changed without removal of engine from chassis.

Flywheel, with renewable starter ring gear, spigoted on rear end of crankshaft and retained by six fitted bolts, equally spaced. When refitting flywheel see that T.D.C. mark on rim coincides with mark on crankshaft flange, as flywheel and crankshaft are balanced as assembly. Thrust button pressed into end of shaft takes thrust of fluid flywheel driven member.

INSTRUMENTS AND CONTROLS (CONQUEST)	GEAR POSITIONS AND BONNET CATCH	
1. Ignition switch.	9. Trafficator warning light.	17. Oil pressure warning light.
2. Starter switch.	10. Heater water control.	18. Ignition warning light.
3. Choke control.	11. Hand throttle.	19. Clock.
4. Lighting switch.	12. Heater motor rheostat.	20. Quadrant, showing gear positions.
5. Petrol reserve.	13. Speedometer.	21. Gear selector lever.
6. Screenwiper switch.	14. Petrol gauge.	22. Bonnet lock (see sketch showing method of releasing two safety catches, one either side).
7. Panel lamp rheostat.	15. Ammeter.	
8. Main beam warning light.	16. Water temperature gauge.	

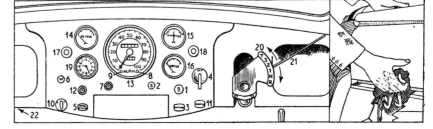

Details of the oil pump, oil filter, piston and con rod group, manifolds and alternative air cleaners are shown below and on the right

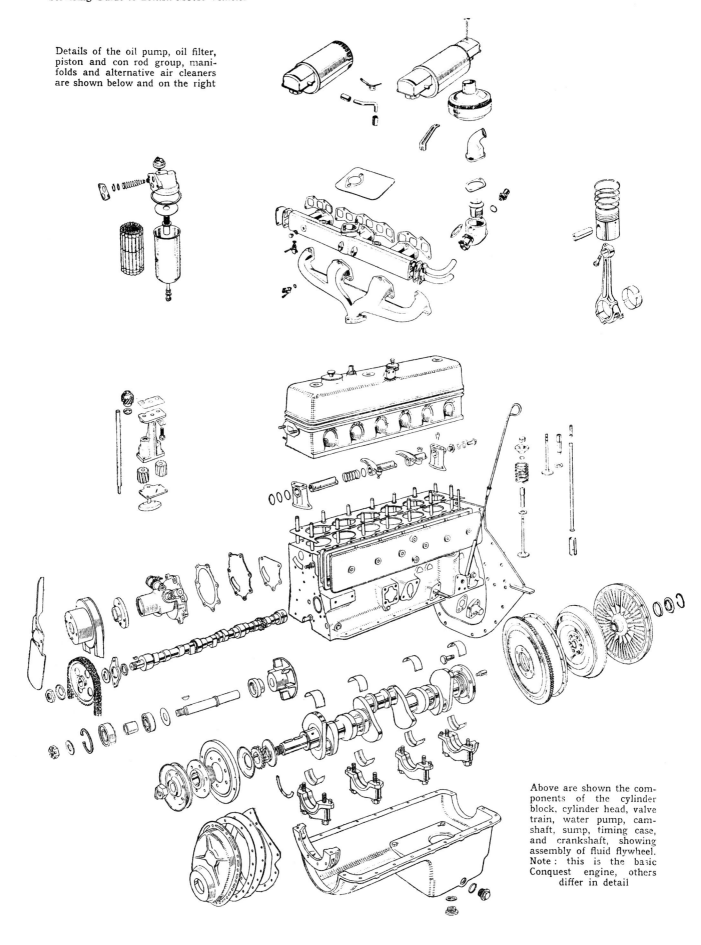

Above are shown the components of the cylinder block, cylinder head, valve train, water pump, camshaft, sump, timing case, and crankshaft, showing assembly of fluid flywheel. Note: this is the basic Conquest engine, others differ in detail

Thrust washer, timing sprocket and pulley pressed on to front end of crankshaft, with oil thrower between sprocket and pulley, keyed with two flat Woodruff keys and retained by hand starter dog nut. Pulley hub passes through scroll in housing pressed into timing cover from inside. Pulley has $\frac{3}{8}$in UNF draw holes.

To remove sump, engine must be removed from chassis.

Connecting Rods

Big ends thin steel-backed, white metal-lined shells located by tabs. Big ends split diagonally, caps located by hollow dowels. Fit with caps towards near (camshaft) side.

Pistons

Aluminium alloy, split skirt. Supplied in two size grades: A suits bore 3·0000-3·0003in, B suits bore 2·9997-3·0000in. Three weight grades: P is lightest (11oz 15dr—12oz 2dr with pin); Q is 12oz 2dr—12oz 5dr; R 12oz 5dr—12oz 9dr. Size and weight grades used for production only, not available for oversizes. Fit with split towards camshafts, with pinch bolt fixing on opposite side.

Big ends will pass through bores. Remove and assemble through top.

Camshaft

Duplex roller chain drive with spring link fastening. Camshaft sprocket keyed with Woodruff key and retained by nut on end of shaft. Camshaft runs in four white metal-lined steel bushes pressed into crankcase. End float controlled by thrust plate between sprocket and shoulder on shaft, bolted to crankcase.

To retime valves, turn crankshaft to T.D.C. 1/6 (mark on flywheel visible through hole in bell-housing and trap in gear box cowl). Keyway will then be at "6 o'clock." One dot on crankshaft sprocket to register between two dots on camshaft sprocket in line with lubricator. Fit chain. No adjustment for timing.

Valves

Overhead, not interchangeable. Inlet larger than exhaust. Split cone cotter fixing. Spring ring on stem below collar. Single springs (double springs Roadster, Coupé and Century).

Valve guides not interchangeable, shouldered. Press in with spring seat washer under shoulder.

Two inserts for Roadster, Coupé and Century (exhaust and inlet).

Renewable exhaust valve seat inserts pressed into head. Replacement inserts supplied slightly oversize to maintain interference. To remove old insert, break out with chisel with alum. alloy head, heat in oven to temp. of 250°F and extract with an expanding puller. Do not chisel; this will damage head. Also heat to fit oversize inserts.

Tappets and Rockers

Barrel tappets sliding directly in crankcase. Remove through side opening. Gauze thimbles in tappet chamber to sump drain holes.

Rocker shaft carried in six pillars and located by setscrew in rear pillar, fed through pipe from rear camshaft bearing.

Rockers are inclined left- and right-handed and fit on either side of each pillar. Rockers of adjacent cylinders separated by spring with washers at either end.

Push rods cannot be extracted with rockers in position.

Lubrication

Gear pump in sump, flange-bolted to bottom of crankcase. Driven from camshaft through skew gear and loose shaft. Flats on lower end of shaft engage with pump driving gear. Shaft, with skew gear keyed (Woodruff key) and pressed on until shaft is just below slot in skew gear; length of shaft to thrust face of skew gear 8.2in. Runs in flanged bronze bush in crankcase and directly in oil pump body; thrust washer between skew gear and upper bush.

Oil drawn from well in sump (no strainer—strainer on Century Coupé and Roadster) and delivered through drilling in body and crankcase to Tecalemit full flow filter bolted to near side of crankcase. Renewable element type FG 2312. For access to element, disconnect oil pressure switch wire and detach body.

Non-adjustable spring-loaded plunger relief valve in side of crankcase behind

SPECIAL TOOLS

	Part No.
Hub drawer	T620-3-1
Front hub bearing outer race drift	T620-3-2
Stub axle bush extractor (press tool)	T620-3-3
Torsion bar setting tool	T620-S18-1
Bus bar height gauge	GDL 35285-85-1

NUT TIGHTENING TORQUE DATA

	Bolt Size	Torque lb ft
Cylinder head* (cast iron) ...	$\frac{7}{16}$in	35 40
Main bearings	$\frac{1}{2}$in	50 57
Big ends	$\frac{3}{8}$in	30 35
Rear spring U bolts	$\frac{7}{16}$in	35 40
Flywheel flange bolts	$\frac{1}{2}$in	50 57

* Century, Coupé and Roadster, aluminium alloy. Same torque.

BALL AND ROLLER BEARING DATA

Taper Roller Bearings	Part No.	Int. dia. Width	Ext. dia. (in or mm)
Front hub bearing (inner)	2698 2631	1.1250	2.615
Front hub bearing (outer)	1755 729	.875	2.240
Rear axle hub bearings ..	3—1+A—025—3	—	—

MODEL IDENTIFICATION DATA

	Type Number		Chassis Number
	R.h.d.	L.h.d.	
Conquest ...	DJ250	DJ251	82,500-84,999
Century ...	DJ256	DJ257	90,950-91,449
Coupe ...	DJ252	DJ253	87,550-87,799
Roadster ...	DJ254	DJ255	90,450-90,949

GENERAL DATA

	Conquest
Wheelbase	8ft 8in
Track: front	4ft 4in
rear	4ft 4in
Turning circle	34ft 0in
Ground clearance*	7in
Tyre size†	6.70—15
Overall length‡	14ft $9\frac{1}{4}$in
Overall width	5ft 6in
Overall height§	5ft 5in
Weight (dry)‖	$27\frac{1}{4}$ cwt

* Roadster $6\frac{1}{2}$in.
† Roadster 6.50 — 15in.
‡ Century and Coupé 14ft $10\frac{3}{4}$in — Roadster 14ft 10in.
§ Coupé 5ft $2\frac{3}{4}$in — Roadster 4ft 10in.
‖ Century 27cwt — Coupé $27\frac{1}{4}$cwt — Roadster $27\frac{3}{4}$ cwt.

ENGINE DATA

No. of cylinders	6
Bore × stroke: mm	76.2 × 88.9
in	3 × $3\frac{1}{2}$
Capacity: cc	2433
cu in	148.4
R.A.C. rated h.p.	21.6
Max. b.h.p. at r.p.m.*	75 at 4000 r.p.m.
Max. torque at r.p.m.†	124 lb/ft at 2000 r.p.m.
Compression ratio‡	6.6 : 1, later 7 : 1 (with steel gasket)

* Century 100 at 4000 r.p.m.—Coupé 100 at 4400 r.p.m.
† Century and Coupé 130 lb/ft at 2500 r.p.m.
‡ Century, Coupé and Roadster 7.75 : 1.

CRANKSHAFT AND CON. RODS

	Main bearings	Crankpins
Diameter	2.250-2.2495in	2.0015-2.001in
Length	1.25in	1.2-1.198in

Running clearance:	
main bearings	.0005-.002in
big ends	.0015in
End float: main bearings ...	.002in
Side clearance: big ends ...	.012-.008in
Undersizes	.010, .020, .030, .040in
Con. rod centres	6.5in
No. of teeth on starter ring gear/pinion	113/10

PISTONS AND RINGS

Clearance (skirt) ...	.0012-.0005in
Oversizes	.010in, .020in
Weight without rings with pin	11 oz 15 dr
Gudgeon pin:	
diameter	$\frac{7}{8}$in
fit in piston ...	Thumb push at room temp.
fit in con. rod ...	Cotter clamped
Compression height ...	1.800±.002in

	Compression	Oil Control
No. of rings	3	1
Gap	.009-.014in	.009-.014in
Side clearance in grooves	.001-.003in	.0015-.003in
Width of rings ...	.0625-.0615in	.1875-.1865in

CAMSHAFT

No. of bearings ...	4
Bearing journal:	
diameter	1.748in
length:	
front and rear ...	1.15in
intermediate ...	.8in
Bearing clearance ...	
Timing chain:	
pitch	$\frac{3}{8}$in
No. of links ...	58

VALVES

	Inlet	Exhaust
Head diameter ...	1.4375in*	1.3125in*
Stem diameter ...	.312in	.312in
Face angle	30°	30°

	Inner (Century and Coupé only)	Outer (all models)
Spring length: free ...	1.29in†	1.93in
fitted ...	1.17in†	1.75in
at load	—	—

* Century, Coupé and Roadster—Head dia: inlet: 1.562in exhaust: 1.437in
† Inner valve spring for Roadster—free length: 1.71in; fitted length: 1.55in.

Diagram showing order of tightening of cylinder head nuts (see "Nut Tightening Torque Data").

Servicing Guide to British Motor Vehicles

filter, retained by "top hat" cover flange-bolted to crankcase. Oil pressure 40lb at normal speed. Green warning light will show below 10lb/sq in.

Cooling System

Pump and fan. Bellows thermostat in water outlet elbow. System pressurized to 4lb/sq in. Pump has carbon and rubber seal unit.

Adjust fan belt by swinging dynamo until belt has ¾in movement either way on top run. Outside diameter of fan belt is 44¼in.

TRANSMISSION

Fluid Flywheel

Open circuit type, using engine oil. Only attention needed is topping up every 3,000 miles. Two combined filler and level plugs on opposite sides. Either can be used. *Flywheel must be topped up only when cold.*

For access, take up carpet and open inspection trap in gearbox cowl. Turn flywheel until plug appears opposite lower hole in bell-housing. Add oil until it overflows.

Gearbox

Four-speed epicyclic self-changing, with preselector.

To adjust gearbox for slip, select each gear in turn and pump pedal about twelve times. If this does not stop slip-ping, remove top cover, exposing adjusters for each brake band. Adjustment takes place automatically each time gear is dis-engaged, when heel of adjuster ring strikes pin, and wrapping action of spring turns nut.

Degree of automatic adjustment governed by setting of adjuster stop screws on brake bands. Excessive adjust-ment may tend to reduce toggle action and cause slipping of brake bands. Select gear which is slipping, and mark adjuster nut with a pencil. Pump gear pedal until nut stops turning (it moves only slightly each time pedal is moved). If gear still slips, toggle action must be increased. Unhook spring round adjuster nut, select and engage another gear, and unscrew adjuster nut one turn. Unlock adjuster stop screw, screw in half a turn and lock. Select and engage gear which is being adjusted, refit spring on round nut, and pump pedal until it stops turning.

When adjusting 1st or reverse gear, engage 2nd, 3rd or top. Do not select neutral, as this partially engages both 1st and reverse. Interlock plungers hold all gears out.

If gear engagement is harsh, toggle action must be decreased. Screw stop screw out one full turn and pump pedal until nut stops turning.

It is possible to miss a gear on selector, when bus bar fails to engage a strut, and bus bar spring "takes charge," forcing gear engaging pedal further back than usual. Considerable force will be needed to press pedal back, but no harm will be done.

To remove gearbox and bell-housing assembly, leaving engine in place, take out front seats and remove brake and "clutch" pedal stalks from levers. Dis-connect accelerator pedal rod, remove gearbox cowl and toeboards on both sides. Disconnect control linkage and speedo drive from gearbox, and remove starter and front exhaust pipe.

Unless car is over pit or on ramp, raise both ends so that bumpers are 24in from ground. Remove propeller shaft com-pletely. Support engine under sump, and detach rear mounting cross-member from cruciform members. Support gearbox on trolley jack and take out bell-housing flange bolts. Draw gearbox back clear of flywheel and lower to ground, rear end first.

To dismantle gearbox, take out rear cover setscrews, and extract driven shaft, rear ball bearing, cover, oil seal and driv-ing flange assembly by tapping flange. Detach large top cover and selector cover on side. Release bus bar spring (small cover on top of box behind large cover) by slackening four setscrews evenly. Pick out spring, guide and bucket.

Unhook adjuster springs, unscrew round nuts, lift out rings and tabies, and remove strut and thrust pad assemblies. Take out eight ⅜in setscrews and nine ¼in setscrews holding gearbox to bell-housing,

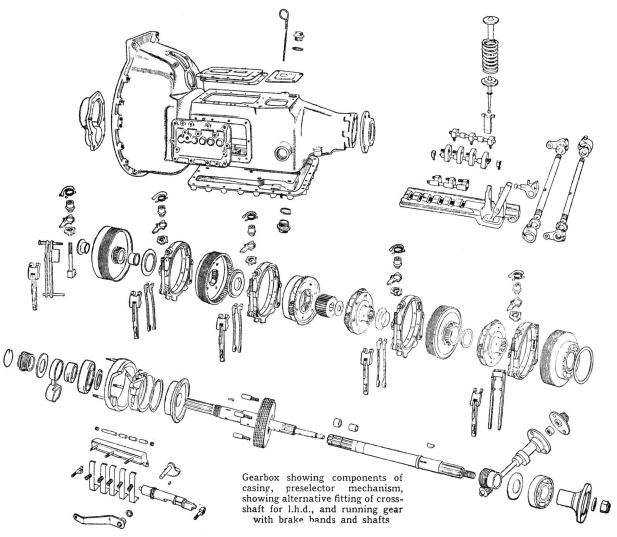

Gearbox showing components of casing, preselector mechanism, showing alternative fitting of cross-shaft for l.h.d., and running gear with brake bands and shafts

DAIMLER CONQUEST

place bell-housing face downwards and break joint by tapping with hide mallet. Lift gearbox, making sure that top gear push rod is tucked into recess in actuating ring and in line with recess in gearbox, and continue until gearbox, with brake band and bus bar assembly, is clear of bell-housing and running gear assembly. Reverse gear drum may stay in box with centre ball bearing, and can be tapped out to front. Note adjusting washer behind bearing.

Running gear components—drums and epicyclic trains—can be picked off until only driving shaft, top gear operating ring and clutch assembly, and front cover and oil pump are left. Unscrew ring-nut (L.H. thread) on driving shaft (locked by spring ring) and detach oil pump housing. Draw off oil thrower ring, plunger, oscillating cylinder and eccentric (Woodruff key), and tap shaft out of front cover and ball bearing, with clutch plate assembly (riveted on). Brake band and bus bar assembly mounted on bottom cover can then be removed from gearbox.

To assemble gearbox place clutch thrust plate and ball thrust bearing on driving shaft, with return springs and plungers in clutch driving member. See that thrust ring is in top gear actuating ring so that it bears on thrust bearing, and that adjusting washer is against shoulder on shaft. Insert shaft into front bearing and cover assembly, and assemble pump eccentric (side marked "front" outwards), plunger, oil thrower and pump body. Tighten nut, making sure that oil return thread is clear of pump body.

Assemble running gear on driving shaft, reversing order of dismantling and noting carefully position of thrust washers and bushes. Check clearance between drums, and renew bushes if necessary. Clearance limits are: Between 1st and reverse .005-.025in; between 1st and 2nd .003-.048in; between 2nd and 3rd .008-.019in.

Check depth of gearbox against height of running gear, and use adjusting washer (.020, .036 or .064in thick) to give .010-.015in end float. Stick adjusting washer in box with grease, and fit top gear rod between top gear hooks (this cannot be done after running gear is in place).

Lower gearbox and brake assembly on to running gear. Assemble struts and automatic adjuster mechanisms. Insert bus bar spring, tightening four setscrews evenly. When assembly is complete, operate bus bar lever several times in each gear to make up automatic adjustment. If new parts have been fitted, height of bus bar in each gear should be checked and, if necessary, set by adjuster nut. special gauge available. Dimensions from top face of gearbox to bottom of bus bar groove should be: Reverse, 5.53in; 1st, 5.58in; 2nd, 5.85in; 3rd, 6.09in; top, 6.00in.

Rear Axle

Salisbury 3 HA hypoid bevel drive, semi-floating shafts. Final drive housing integral with axle tubes, rear cover detachable.

To remove axle from car, jack up rear, disconnect brake linkage, shock absorbers, propeller shaft and spring U-bolts. Lift axle out sideways through springs.

Construction and servicing procedure are exactly as for rear axle fitted on Lanchester Leda previously described. Setting mark on face of pinion is bottom figure of four sets of figures.

CHASSIS

Brakes

Snail cam adjustment for front brakes. Jack up car and tighten each adjuster (one for each shoe) until shoe is firmly against drum, then back off until wheel is free. Square ended adjusters for rear brakes. Tighten and back off until wheel is free.

Rear Springs

Semi-elliptic. Spring eyes and shackles have threaded bronze bushes (all interchangeable) pressed in. On Century, Coupé and Roadster models Silentbloc bushes are fitted. Threaded bolts fit in shackle and anchorage brackets, heads to outside locked against step in bracket. Felt washers on either side of spring eyes and shackles.

Front Suspension

Independent, laminated torsion bars.

To remove torsion bar, jack up front end, placing stands beneath side members to take weight. Wheels remain on the ground. Fit tool No. T620-S 18-1 at back of torsion bars so that clamp brackets are approx. 3in from rear adaptors. Mark front and rear adaptors so that bars may be replaced in original positions. Remove nuts from bolts holding rear adaptor of torsion bar, rotating adjuster turnbuckle so that clamp brackets move inwards along threads until rear adaptor mounting bolts can be freed. Rotate adjuster turnbuckle in opposite direction until torsion bar is completely unwound. Remove clamp bracket and front adaptor securing bolts, tap rear adaptor clear of chassis frame. Torsion bar can now be withdrawn. If both bars are to be removed it will be necessary to refit one in position after unwinding to act as anchor for adjuster when releasing second bar.

Replacement of torsion bars is a reversal of above procedure. Torsion bars may be adjusted individually using special tool mentioned earlier. Proceed as for removal of bar removing front adaptor securing bolts, turning the adaptor the required number of holes and in the predetermined direction. To raise car ½in on near side move front adaptor one hole in an anti-clockwise direction and rear adaptor one hole in the same direction, both adaptors being viewed from the *back* of the car. Adjusting off-side suspension, it will be necessary to turn adaptors in a clockwise direction to obtain similar adjustment on that assembly. Reversal of these turning directions lowers car on suspension. When car is equipped for road, distance from lower edge of front cross member to ground should be 7½in approx.

Shims are provided to adjust king pin end float in thicknesses of .005, .010 and .015 for adjustment.

Hub bearings adjusted by castellated nut; adjust so that bearing is free when outer nut is tightened fully (max. .004in end play).

Camber angle adjustment made by addition or removal of shims between chassis frame and upper transverse link bracket. Removal of shims decreases angle, addition increases angle.

Three-piece track rod, with idler arm. Before adjusting track check that idler arm is parallel to drop arm when steering is halfway between locks (upright spoke of steering wheel perpendicular). Adjust centre section if necessary. *Track adjustment should be made on outer rods only* (threaded r.h. and l.h.), *and both rods should be same length.*

CHASSIS DATA

CLUTCH

Daimler Fluid Flywheel fitted to all Models.

GEARBOX

Type	Epicyclic, pre-selector
No. of forward speeds	4
Final ratios: 1st	17.47 : 1
(except 2nd	10.05 : 1
Roadster) 3rd	6.71 : 1
4th	4.56 : 1
Rev.	17.46 : 1
Propeller shaft	
Make	Hardy Spicer
Journal and needle bearing package	K5, L4

FINAL DRIVE

Type	Hypoid bevel
Crown wheel/bevel pinion teeth	41/9*

* Roadster—41/11

BRAKES

Type	Girling hydro-mech.
Drum diameter	11in
Lining: length	10¾in
width	1¾in†
thickness	$\frac{3}{16}$in
Hyd. cylinder diameter:	
master	⅞in
wheel	⅞in
No. of rivets per shoe ...	12

† Century, Coupé and Roadster—2¼in

SPRINGS

	Front	Rear
Length (eye centres, laden)	—	46in
Width	1.52in	1.75-1.78in
Thickness	.264in	.20in
No. of leaves	5	10
Free camber length ...	—	6½±¼in‡
Loaded camber at load ...	—	½±⅛in neg. at 798lb load

‡ Century and Roadster—Free camber length 5.3 and 4.3in±¼in .8in±⅛in at loads of 748lb and 670lb respectively.

SHOCK ABSORBERS

Make	Girling
Type	Telescopic DAS 435*
Service	Replacement

* Century, Coupé and Roadster—type DAS 5/45NF

STEERING BOX

Make	Bishop
Type	Cam and Peg TQ
Adjustments:	
Column end float ...	Shims
Cross shaft end float ...	Grub screw and locknut
Mesh	Grub screw and locknut

FRONT-END SERVICE DATA

Castor	Nil
Camber	1½°
King pin inclination ...	8°
Toe-in	⅛in
No. of turns lock to lock ...	3¼†
Adjustments: castor ...	—
camber ...	Shims
toe-in ...	See text

† Roadster—2¾.

Chassis Lubrication

Luvax thermal system, consisting of reservoir, expansion chamber mounted near exhaust down pipes, and pipe lines branching to metering valves.

If any pipe is disconnected, system must be primed by pressure pump connected to three-way junction just below expansion chamber.

Trailer Attachment

No special provision for trailer bracket. Towing capacity 30 cwt.

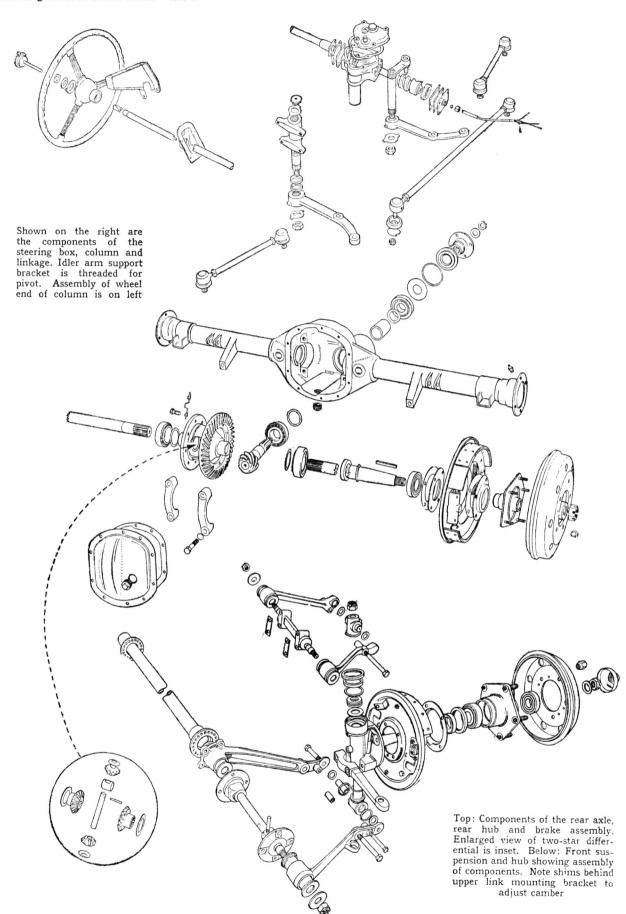

Shown on the right are the components of the steering box, column and linkage. Idler arm support bracket is threaded for pivot. Assembly of wheel end of column is on left

Top: Components of the rear axle, rear hub and brake assembly. Enlarged view of two-star differential is inset. Below: Front suspension and hub showing assembly of components. Note shims behind upper link mounting bracket to adjust camber

TUNE-UP DATA

Firing order	...	1, 5, 3, 6, 2, 4
Tappet clearance, hot: inlet and exhaust	...	.013in
No. of flywheel teeth	...	113
Valve timing:* inlet opens	...	17° BTDC
inlet closes	...	55° ABDC
exhaust opens	...	50° BBDC
exhaust closes	...	22° ATDC
Standard ignition timing	...	9° BTDC
Location of timing mark	...	Flywheel and cover
Distributor: type and service No.	...	DM6 40423A DM6 40424 Roadster and Century
Advance range (dist. deg.): centrif.	...	14½°–16½°
vacuum	...	8°–10°
Advance starts (dist. r.p.m.)	...	300
Max. advance (dist. r.p.m.)	...	2,000
Cam angle	...	35°±2°
Contact spring tension	...	20–24 oz
Contact set No.	...	420197
Contact breaker gap	...	.014in–.016in
Condenser: capacity	...	0.18–0.23 mf
Plugs: make	...	Lodge
type	...	HLN
size	...	14 mm
gap	...	.020in

Carburetter : make†	...	Zenith S.U.
type†	...	42V.15 H.6
Settings: Choke	...	29 1⅜in.‡
Main jet	...	90
Needle (standard)	...	SW
Comp. jet	...	105
Progression jet	...	170
Idle jet	...	55
High speed bleed	...	1.9 mm
Part throttle air bleed	...	4.0 mm
Pump jet	...	60
Pump stroke	...	long
Needle valve seat	...	2.5 mm
Air cleaner (Consort): home	...	AC7222656
export (oil bath)	...	AC7222655
Fuel pump: make	...	AC
type	...	UE 152750
pressure	...	1lb

* Century and Coupé: Inlet opens 13° BTDC; inlet closes 65° ABDC; exhaust opens 55° BBDC; exhaust closes 21° ATDC.

Roadster: Inlet opens 13° BTDC ; inlet closes 65° ABDC; exhaust opens 55° BBDC; exhaust closes 23° ATDC.

† Century, Coupé and Roadster, S.U. twin.

‡ Coupé 1⅛in.

ELECTRICAL TEST DATA

Battery (all models)		
model	...	GTW 9A/2
voltage	...	12
No. of plates per cell	...	9
capacity	...	51 ah at 10 hr. rate
Spec. gravity: up to 80° F	...	1.280–1.300
(in climate 80°–100° F ranges) over 100° F	...	1.250–1.270
	...	1.220–1.240
Dynamo		
model	...	C39 PV-2
service no. (all models)	...	22258D
rotation (comm. end)	...	Anti-clockwise
cut-in volts at r.p.m.	...	13 at 1050–1200 r.p.m.
output amps at r.p.m.	...	19 amps at 2,000–2,150 r.p.m.
field resistance	...	6.2 ohms
brush tension	...	22–25 oz
Control box		
model	...	RB 106/1
service no. (all models)	...	37138 D
cut-out: cut-in voltage	...	12.7–13.3
cut-out voltage	...	9–10
regulator voltage: 10° C (50° F)	...	15.9–16.5
20° C (68° F)	...	15.6–16.2
30° C (86° F)	...	15.3–15.9
40° C (104° F)	...	15.0–15.6
Starter		
model	...	M 418 G
service no. (all models)	...	25521 D
rotation (comm. end)	...	Anti-clockwise
lock torque (lb/ft-amps-volts)	...	17 lb/ft at 440–460 amps and 7.4–7 volts
torque at 1,000 r.p.m.	...	8 lb/ft at 250–270 amps
brush tension	...	30–40 oz
Coil		
model	...	B12
service no. (all models)	...	45012 D
stall current	...	3.3 amps (approx.)
running current	...	1.4 amps at 1000 r.p.m.

ADDITIONAL ELECTRICAL DATA
(Lucas Equipment)

	Model	Service No.
Headlamps. Right-hand drive (all models)	F700	51336A
Side lamps (Conquest and Century)	488	53210A
Side lamps (Roadster)	513	52145B
Stop tail lamps (Conquest and Century)	464	53199E
Stop tail and flasher lamps (Roadster)	538	53372A
No. plate and reverse lamp (Conquest and Century)	469	53161B
No. plate lamp (Roadster)	467/2	53093B
Reverse lamp (Roadster)	539	53378A
Fog lamp (Conquest)	FFT462	55043E
Direction indicator lamp (Roadster)	488	52246A
Starter push (all models)	SS8	31115
Starter solenoid switch (all models)	ST950	76411D
Dipper switch (all models)	FS22	31284
Lighting switch (all models)	PRS5	31303
Ignition switch (all models)	S45	31287B
Screenwiper switch	PS16	31113
Screen wiper (motor)	DR1	75245A
Horns: High note	WT614	69011J
Low note	WT614	69012J
Trafficators (Conquest and Century)	SF80	54044D
Flasher unit (when fitted)	FL3	35003A
Flasher relay (when fitted)	DB10	33117D
Fuse unit (all models)	SF6	033239
Contains 2—35-amp fuses		

BULBS

	Voltage	Wattage	No.
Headlamps. Dip left	12	42/36	354
Sidelamps (all models)	12	6	207
Stop tail lamps	12	6/18	361
No. plate and reverse lamp (Conquest and Century)	12	4	222
No. plate lamp (Roadster)	12	21	382
No. plate lamp (Roadster)	12	4	222
Reverse lamp (Roadster)	12	21	382
Foglamp (Conquest)	12	38	325
Direction indicator lamp (Roadster)	12	21	382
Trafficator (Conquest and Century)	12	3	256
Ignition warning light (all models)	12	2.2	87
Panel lights (all models)	12	6	—
Interior light (Century)	12	4	222

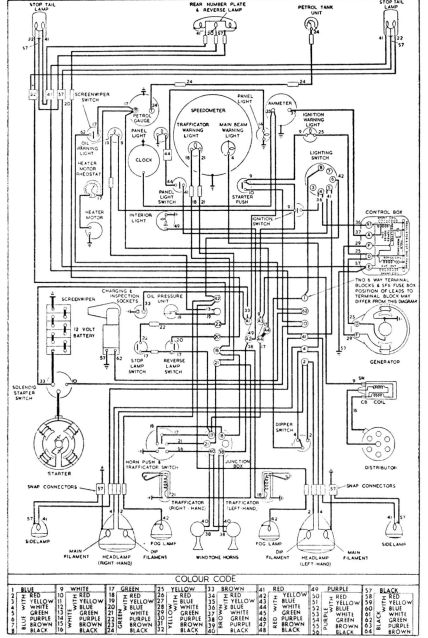

COLOUR CODE

1 BLUE	9 WHITE	17 GREEN	25 YELLOW	33 BROWN	41 RED	49 PURPLE	57 BLACK
2 RED	10 RED	18 RED	26 RED	34 RED	42 YELLOW	50 RED	58 RED
3 YELLOW	11 YELLOW	19 YELLOW	27 YELLOW	35 YELLOW	43 YELLOW	51 YELLOW	59 YELLOW
4 WHITE	12 BLUE	20 BLUE	28 BLUE	36 BLUE	44 BLUE	52 BLUE	60 BLUE
5 GREEN	13 GREEN	21 WHITE	29 WHITE	37 WHITE	45 GREEN	53 WHITE	61 WHITE
6 PURPLE	14 PURPLE	22 PURPLE	30 PURPLE	38 PURPLE	46 PURPLE	54 GREEN	62 GREEN
7 BROWN	15 BROWN	23 BROWN	31 BROWN	39 BROWN	47 BROWN	55 BROWN	63 PURPLE
8 BLACK	16 BLACK	24 BLACK	32 BLACK	40 BLACK	48 BLACK	56 BLACK	64 BROWN

Diagram (for Conquest only) by permission of Joseph Lucas, Ltd.

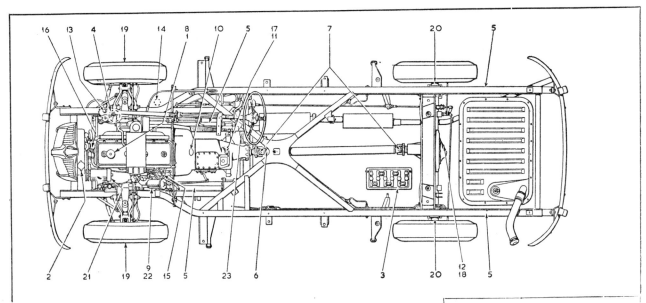

KEY TO MAINTENANCE DIAGRAM

DAILY
1. Engine sump } Top up
2. Radiator

MONTHLY
3. Battery } Top up
4. Chassis lubrication reservoir
5. Springs and torsion bars—Spray with penetrating oil

EVERY 1,000 MILES
6. Propeller shaft splines } Oil gun
7. Propeller shaft universal joints

EVERY 3,000 MILES
8. Engine sump—Drain and refill
9. Engine oil filter—Clean element in petrol.
10. Fluid flywheel
11. Gearbox
12. Rear axle } Top up
13. Steering box
14. Brake fluid reservoir
15. Distributor—Oil shaft bearing, auto advance and contact breaker pivot. Grease cam
16. Water pump—Grease gun

EVERY 6,000 MILES
17. Gearbox } Drain and refill
18. Rear axle

EVERY 12,000 MILES
19. Front hubs—Repack with grease
20. Rear hubs—Grease gun
21. Dynamo—Refill lubricator with H.M.P. grease

EVERY 18,000 MILES
22. Engine oil filter—Renew element (Tecalemit FG 2312)
23. Speedo drive—Extract cable and smear with grease

FILL-UP DATA

				Litres
Engine sump	...	...	10pt	5.7
Gearbox	...	...	5½pt	3.3
Rear axle	...	...	2½pt	1.4
Fluid flywheel		...	8pt	4.5
Cooling system	...	...	18pt*	10.3
Fuel tank	...	...	15 gall †	68
Chassis lubrication tank	...	1¼pt	.71
Tyre pressures: front	...	24lb/sqin	
	rear		24lb/sqin	

* Roadster—17pt (9.7 litres)
† Roadster—16 gall (73 litres)

DRAINING POINTS

Left: Radiator drain tap on extension pipe on off side, accessible from below. Right: Manifold drain tap with cylinder block drain tap below, on off side at rear of engine. Remove filler cap to speed draining. All taps shown in closed position. *Note: Cooling system is pressurized*

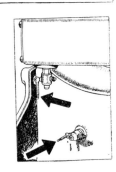

RECOMMENDED LUBRICANTS

		S.A.E. No.	Daimler	Wakefield	Vacuum	Shell-Mex	Esso	B.P. Energol
Engine	Above 90° F	40	—	—	—	—	—	—
	90-32° F	30	Solvent Process	Castrol XL	Mobiloil A	X-100 30	Essolube 30	Energol S.A.E. 30
	Below 32° F	20	—	—	—	—	—	—
Fluid Flywheel, Gearbox		30	Solvent Process	Castrol XL	Mobiloil A	X-100 30	Essolube 30	Energol S.A.E. 30
Rear Axle		90	Heavy Gear Oil	Castrol Hypoy	Mobilube GX 90	Spirax 90 EP	Esso Expee Compound 90	Energol S.A.E. 90
Steering Box		140	—	Castrol Hypoy	Mobilube C90	Spirax 140 EP	Esso Gear Oil 140	Energol EP S.A.E. 140
Chassis Lubrication System		—	Luvax Bijur Chassis Oil	Castrol ST	Mobilube C90	Spirax 140 EP	Esso Gear Oil 90 Light	Energol S.A.E. 90
Front Wheel Hubs, Dynamo		—	RB Grease	Castrolease Heavy	Mobil Hub Grease	Retinax RB	Esso Grease	Belmoline C
Rear Springs		—	Oil Penetrating	Penetrating Oil	Mobil Spring Oil	Donax P	Penetrating Oil	Penetrating Oil
Brake Fluid					Brake fluid Crimson			
Shock Absorbers					Girling Damper Oil (Thin)			